ROUTLEDGE LIBRARY EDITIONS:
INTERNATIONAL TRADE POLICY

Volume 6

CONSTRAINTS AND COMPROMISES

CONSTRAINTS AND COMPROMISES

Trade Policy in a Democracy: The Case of the
U.S.-Israel Free Trade Area

ORIT FRENKEL

Routledge
Taylor & Francis Group

LONDON AND NEW YORK

First published in 1990 by Garland Publishing, Inc.

This edition first published in 2018
by Routledge
2 Park Square, Milton Park, Abingdon, Oxon OX14 4RN

and by Routledge
711 Third Avenue, New York, NY 10017

Routledge is an imprint of the Taylor & Francis Group, an informa business

British Library Cataloguing in Publication Data
A catalogue record for this book is available from the British Library

ISBN: 978-1-138-06323-5 (Set)
ISBN: 978-1-315-14339-2 (Set) (ebk)
ISBN: 978-1-138-10675-8 (Volume 6) (hbk)
ISBN: 978-1-315-10141-5 (Volume 6) (ebk)

Publisher's Note
The publisher has gone to great lengths to ensure the quality of this reprint but
points out that some imperfections in the original copies may be apparent.

Disclaimer
The publisher has made every effort to trace copyright holders and would welcome
correspondence from those they have been unable to trace.

FOREIGN ECONOMIC POLICY OF THE UNITED STATES

Constraints and Compromises:
Trade Policy in a Democracy
The Case of the U.S.-Israel Free Trade Area

ORIT FRENKEL

GARLAND PUBLISHING, INC.
NEW YORK & LONDON • *1990*

Library of Congress Cataloging-in-Publication Data

Frenkel, Orit.
Constraints and compromises: trade policy in a democracy: the case of
the U.S.-Israel Free Trade Area/ Orit Frenkel.
p. cm.—(Foreign economic policy of the United States)
Originally presented as the author's thesis (Ph.D.)—Johns Hopkins
University, 1988.
Includes bibliographical references.
ISBN 0-8240-7464-5 (alk. paper)
1. United States—Commercial policy. 2. Free trade—United States.
3. Free trade—Israel. 4. United States—Commerce—Israel. 5. Israel—
Commerce—United States. 6. Tariff—United States. 7. Tariff—Israel.
I. Title. II. Series.
HF1455.F746   1990
382'.095694073—dc20   90-2998

Printed on acid-free, 250-year-life paper.
Manufactured in the United States of America

PREFACE

This study stems from my three and one-half years at the Office of the U.S. Trade Representative where I had the opportunity to view and participate in the trade policy process first hand. This experience, together with a Congressional fellowship, gave me an insight into the relationship between the Executive branch and the Congress in making trade policy and negotiating trade agreements. I gained an appreciation of the constraints faced by both branches of government, and the compromises necessary to achieve any goal, particularly one as significant as the U.S.-Israel Free Trade Area. The six months that I spent in Israel, under the auspices of the Dayan Center at Tel Aviv University, gave me an understanding of the difficulties our governmental process imposes on a country trying to negotiate with the United States. The purpose of this study is to examine the impact of U.S. domestic political constraints on the negotiation of trade agreements. Because our government is a democracy, these political constraints will continue to be present. Nevertheless, I hope that by better understanding the influence of domestic political constraints on trade agreements, U.S. policymakers will be better equipped to negotiate trade agreements that balance economic considerations with political feasibility.

This study demonstrates that there are strong incentives in the U.S. trade policy system for maintaining trade barriers for industries that have traditionally been protected, even in the context of a trade-liberalizing agreement. The negotiation of the U.S.-Israel FTA was fraught with domestic obstacles and political resistance, despite the fact that the economic impact of the agreement was expected to be minimal. This study illustrates how domestic political pressures led to a free trade area which was intended to liberalize bilateral trade completely, but in the end maintained significant barriers to trade.

In the four years since the negotiation of the U.S.-Israel FTA, the study's hypothesis has been born out. The FTA has had no clear impact on the level of trade between the United States and Israel. Israel's exports to the U.S. have actually increased at a slower rate than during the several years preceding the agreement. The FTA's lackluster performance could have been predicted by the fact that each country maintained significant nontariff trade barriers in the context of the FTA. Four years later the U.S. and Israel are still working out many of the nontariff issues that were left unresolved when the FTA was negotiated. On the positive side, these issues have been dealt with constructively, and the negotiation of the U.S.-Israel FTA and the lessons learned laid the groundwork for the U.S.-Canada Free Trade Area negotiations and other bilateral agreements, including one now being contemplated with Mexico.

In completing this study, I have incurred a long list of debts. Since much of this study is based on information obtained from personal interviews, there are a great many people who were generous with their time and frank with their thoughts, and I am indebted to them all. In particular, Nancy Adams spent a great deal of time with me, patiently answering my never-ending questions, and helping me piece the negotiation process together. In addition. I must thank my principal advisors, James Riedel and Joseph Pelzman who were both there when I needed them, knowing when to be supportive and when to be prodding. Most of all, this study is dedicated to my parents, who told me that I could do it, and to Claude, who showed me the way.

Orit Frenkel

Table of Contents

List of Tables and Figures

I. Introduction

The negotiation of the Agreement on the Establishment of a Free Trade Area between the United States of America and the Government of Israel ("the FTA") stands as a remarkable political accomplishment for the U.S. government. It is the first free trade area for the United States and the second for Israel, which has a less comprehensive free trade agreement with the European Economic Community. The FTA addresses tariffs as well as certain nontariff barriers to trade. Its tariff provisions provide for complete elimination of tariffs by both sides by January 1, 1995. Certain of its nontariff provisions go beyond the requirements of any existing international discipline, including a provision regarding trade in services. This study examines the FTA negotiation as a case study of the trade negotiation process.

U.S. trade negotiators must contend with the inevitable constraints of the domestic political system. Under the Constitution, international commercial relations are the province of the Congress. Although the President can negotiate trade agreements with foreign governments, such agreements generally must be acted upon by the

Congress in order to be implemented into U.S. law. Trade agreements are thus influenced by the constituent concerns of the Congress. The implication for trade negotiations is that U.S. negotiators are guided by the necessity of negotiating an agreement that has the greatest chance of passing Congress. This necessity profoundly influences the nature of trade agreements negotiated by the United States.

Over the last fifty years, the U.S. Congress has generally favored free trade and trade liberalization. Yet, members of Congress are usually under political pressure to continue protecting those industries in their districts that are already heavily protected. The result has been that Congressional representatives seek trade liberalizing agreements that maintain import restrictions for protected industries in their districts while promoting tariff-cutting authority for all other industries.[1] Thus, U.S. negotiators try to minimize Congressional opposition to trade agreements by maintaining the existing structure of protection, to the greatest extent possible, within the context of a liberalizing agreement.

---

[1] Robert E. Baldwin, "The Political Economy of Postwar U.S. U.S. Trade Policy", The Bulletin, New York University Graduate School of Business Administration, vol.4, 1976, p. 14.

liberalizing agreement.

The "existing structure of protection" means the extent to which various industries are currently protected by import restrictions relative to each another. Maintaining the existing structure of protection results in a cycle where the industries that are already heavily protected continue to receive more trade protection (or less duty reductions) than industries that are less protected.

The negotiation of the U.S.-Israel FTA was fraught with domestic obstacles and political resistance, despite the fact that the economic impact of the agreement was predicted to be minimal. At the time of the negotiation, only 0.5% of total U.S. imports came from Israel, and 93% of these imports from Israel already entered the United States duty free.[2] Furthermore, the FTA was estimated to result in only a minimal increase in Israel's exports to the United States; one study projected that increase at approximately $15.7 million.[3] Although the FTA's economic significance for

---

[2]U.S. Department of Commerce, Import Monthly, series 145, Washington D.C., 1983.

[3]Joseph Pelzman. "The Impact of the U.S.-Israel Free Trade Area Agreement on Israeli Trade and Employment," The Maurice Falk Institute for Economic Research in Israel, Discussion Paper No. 85.08, Jerusalem, June

the United States was relatively inconsequential, the United States conducted a negotiation intended to preserve many of its existing barriers to trade. The resulting agreement maintained all U.S. quotas. Moreover, it placed almost all of the tariff items in which Israel could potentially increase exports to the United States in the later tariff elimination categories.

While valid economic considerations, such as labor adjustment costs, may sometimes justify the continuing protection of certain industries, in the case of the FTA, the decisions as to which industries to protect were as a result of political pressure, rather than economic considerations. Because the volume of Israel's imports into the United States is so small, the possibility of labor adjustment costs resulting from U.S. tariff elimination is negligible. In fact, the evidence shows that the industries that were protected in the course of the negotiations were those which exercised political power in Congress.

This study examines why the FTA negotiation was politicized, and the impact of the political process on the negotiation of the FTA. It follows the U.S.-Israel FTA

Publishers, 1986. p. 41-42.

from its inception through its implementation, suggesting why the agreement took its final shape, and the process and motivations that determined the final outcome. This sequence of events will be used as a case study to examine the trade negotiation process and the relationship between Congress and the Executive branch in that process.

The negotiation of the U.S.-Israel FTA is a useful case study of a trade negotiation because it includes all of the industrial and agricultural sectors, thus spanning the full spectrum of issues that would be dealt with in a larger negotiation. The negotiation of the U.S.--Israel FTA provides a microcosm of the many political pressures and constraints which play a role in reaching any trade agreement. In addition, it has the advantage of involving just two countries and lasting only fifteen months from commencement to completion, thus facilitating a comprehensive analysis.

This study begins with a review of writings by economists and political scientists on the political economy of trade policy and trade negotiations in the United States. Chapter II examines the economic literature on the determinants of protection, the literature that seeks to explain why certain industries receive more protection from imports than others, and the industry characteristics that contribute to obtaining protection. It then examines the literature that discusses these interindustry differences and how they carry over into trade negotiations. The chapter concludes with a discussion of the political science literature on the political process involved in trade policy, and in particular, the role of pressure groups and the Congress. All of these works are used to develop a framework to analyze the negotiation of the FTA.

Chapter III discusses the economic environment forming the backdrop to the negotiation of the FTA. It examines the bilateral trading relationship between the United States and Israel that existed prior to the FTA, including the barriers to trade, and then discusses how these barriers were, or were not, addressed in the agreement. In order to analyze the potential effect of the FTA, the chapter briefly reviews the economic theory of free trade areas, and then goes on to examine studies that have estimated the economic impact of the FTA. The chapter concludes with a discussion of the potential benefits and limitations of the FTA for both countries.

Chapter IV examines the motivations that led to the negotiation of the FTA, and the policy process that paved the way for its implementation in the United States. The chapter briefly presents a background to U.S. trade policy and the events that led both countries toward the decision to negotiate a free trade area. It then analyzes the role of the Congress in the negotiation of the FTA, as well as the FTA's implementation into U.S. law. The chapter discusses the impact of the report written by the U. S. International Trade Commission (ITC) on the domestic trade policy process and on the negotiations. The chapter ends with a discussion of how pressure groups were involved in informing and influencing the government, and as a result, in the negotiation and implementation of the FTA.

Chapter V analyzes the negotiation process, starting with a discussion of the expectations and objectives with which both the United States and Israel entered into the FTA negotiations. It then traces the evolution of both countries' expectations through the course of the negotiations, and discusses how each country fared in the negotiations.

Chapter VI develops a quantitative model to formally show that the best indicator of how an item was dealt with in the course of the FTA negotiations was the level of protection that item had before the FTA. Using a documentation of the tariff offers made by each country during the negotiation, this chapter develops a model that uses the level of protection (tariff and nontariff barriers) prior to the FTA negotiation as an indication of how negotiators would treat individual products during the course of the FTA negotiations.

The final chapter draws conclusions based upon the analysis of the motivations, the trade policy and negotiation processes, and results of the FTA nego- tiations. This chapter concludes with the implications of this analysis for future trade negotiations and trade policy research.

II.   Literature Review and Theoretical Framework

Before analyzing the negotiation of the U.S.-Israel Free
Trade Area, it is useful to examine the existing
research on trade policy and trade negotiations. This
chapter will discuss the research on the nature of
protection and the trade policy process done by both
political scientists and economists. By drawing on both
bodies of work, it will develop a framework to analyze
the negotiation of the U.S.-Israel FTA.

Although it has always been recognized that politics and
economics are inextricably linked in the making of trade
policy, only recently has a significant amount of
attention been given to their linkage. Economists
traditionally take trade policies as given, and analyze
their economic welfare effects. Over the past decade,
however, a growing number of studies have been under-
taken by economists that deal with the political economy
of protection. These studies have focused predominantly
on the determinants of protection, the alignment of
groups for and against protection, and the differences
in levels of protection between various industries. In
contrast, the political science literature has focused
traditionally on the politics and process of trade
policy, the role of pressure groups in deciding which

industries or groups are protected, and the roles of Congress, bureaucrats, and the President in the trade policy process.

The first part of this chapter examines the economic literature on the determinants of protection. The second section of the chapter discusses the economic literature seeking to explain why certain industries receive more protection from imports than others, and the industry characteristics that contribute to obtaining protection. A discussion of the economic literature examining the impact of these interindustry differences on trade negotiations is followed by the political science literature on the political process involved in trade policy, and in particular, the role of pressure groups and the Congress. In the final section of the chapter, these themes are integrated into a framework for analysis that will be used throughout this study.

A. Economic Theory and the Determinants of Protection

Neoclassical trade theory states that protecting domestic industries from import competition generally lowers a country's real national income, unless the country's trade volume is large enough to have an effect

on world prices.[1] Furthermore, protection is also not
the best way to foster a particular domestic industry.
Economists have been forced to ask why, given these
postulates, nations so often use protection. One answer
is that nations seek to protect industries for noneconomic reasons. In his article on the scientific
tariff, Harry Johnson discusses many noneconomic reasons
for a tariff, including a desire for industrialization,
military preparedness, equitable income distribution, or
a particular way of life.[2] Johnson, however, points out
that the tariff has inefficiency costs and is thus not
the best way to accomplish these ends.

A nation might resort to the use of protection because
of pressures from the political process. Brock and
Magee argue that the more competitive the political
system, the more likely that "political pressures will
force politicians to act less like economic statesmen
concerned with minimizing social costs, and to act
merely as intermediaries between conflicting economic

---

[1]See, for example, Richard E. Caves and Ronald
W. Jones, World Trade and Payments: An Introduction,
(Boston: Little, Brown and Co., 1973).

[2]Harry G. Johnson, "The Cost of Protection and the
Scientific Tariff," Journal of Political Economy,
vol. 68 No. 4., August 1960, p. 327.

groups."[3] They contend that the tariff can be viewed as a price which reflects the "political terms of trade" between small, but well-organized producer groups, and larger, but less organized consumer groups.[4]

While this formulation is new, international trade theory has historically identified groups on both sides of the tariff issue. In 1874, James Cairnes developed a model with all factors of production being industry--specific, and argued that all factors in import--competing industries favor protection, while consumers and those in export industries favor free trade.[5] Later the Stolper-Samuelson model argued that in a two factor economy, the relatively abundant factor will favor free trade, while the relatively scarce factor will favor protection.[6]

A different approach was taken by Albert Breton who analyzed the determinants of protection in a democracy

---

[3]William Brock and Stephen Magee, "Tariff Formation in a Democracy", in eds. John Black and Brian Hindley, Current Issues in Commercial Policy and Diplomacy, (London: Macmillam Press, 1980), p.1.

[4]Ibid.

[5]James E. Cairnes, Some Leading Principles in Political Economy, (London: Macmillan, 1874).

[6]W. Stolper and Paul A. Samuelson, "Protection and Real Wages," Review of Economic Studies, No. 9, November 1941, pp. 58-73.

in terms of a political market for protection, in which
import-competing producers are the demanders of protection and the government is the supplier.[7] Import-
-competing producers are the demanders of protection
because a tariff increases the producer surplus of firms
in the industry. As a result, these producers are
willing to use part of their expected increase in income
to influence legislators to "supply" protection to their
industry.[8]

This analysis assumes that since legislators are
motivated primarily by their desire to remain in office,
they weigh the political pressures for and against an
industry's protection with that goal in mind. The
principal losers from increased tariffs are the product's consumers (and exporters). Although in traditional trade theory, consumer surplus losses due to
tariff increases are greater than producer surplus gain,
the consumer surplus loss is spread over a large and
dispersed group. The gains per producer are greater
than the loss per consumer. As such, producers are able

---

[7]Albert Breton, The Economic Theory of Representative Government, (Chicago: Aldine Publishing Co.,
1974).

[8]Kym Anderson and Robert E. Baldwin, "The Political
Market for Protection in Industrial Countries:
Empirical Evidence," World Bank Staff Working Paper
No.42, Washington D.C., October 1981, p.3.

to coalesce better than consumers, and lobbying activities by consumers are generally ineffective. As a result, an industry seeking protection can often offset opposition to a tariff increase by spending sufficient funds to present the industry's case to elected officials.

Anthony Downs shows that producers are generally better informed than consumers about trade policy.[9] Brock and Magee go a step further to show that producers also supply information to Congress in order to influence their votes.[10] Baldwin's research also bears out the assertion that pressure groups do not cancel each other out.[11] In his statistical analysis of the factors affecting Congressional votes on the 1974 Trade Act, Baldwin confirms that constituent influences are typically from importcompeting industries, rather than from export-oriented industries.

Thus, economic research shows that protection exists, in

---

[9]Anthony Downs, <u>An Economic Theory of Democracy</u>, (New York: Harper and Brothers, 1957) pp. 255-6.

[10]William A. Brock and Stephen P. Magee, "An Economic Theory of Politics: The Case of Tariffs"(mimeographed), 1974, as cited in Baldwin, "The Political Economy of Postwar U.S. U.S. Trade Policy," p. 3.

[11]Baldwin, "The Political Economy of Postwar U.S. Trade Policy."

part, because in some groups (i.e., producers), members stand to gain more and are better informed about their gains from protection, and in other groups (i.e., consumers), individual members stand to lose less and are less informed about their losses. Most importantly in a democracy, the groups that gain from protection are better able to influence the decisions of government officials than the groups that lose from protection.

B. Industry Differences in Obtaining Protection

While the above discussion aims at explaining the existence of protection, another body of economic literature has sought to answer the question of why some industries are more successful in obtaining protection than others. Several key types of models emerge from the economic analysis done on the characteristics contributing to an industry's protection.[12]

Writers such as Olson, Pincus, and Brock and Magee use the common interest or pressure group model to look at the ability of an industry to organize as a political pressure group. Variables used to reflect an industry's

---

[12]Robert E. Baldwin, "Trade Policies in Developed Countries," in eds. R.W. Jones and P.B. Kenen, Handbook of International Economics vol. I, (Amsterdam: North Holland Publishing Co., 1984). p. 574.

ability to organize are the number of firms in an
industry, the degree of its concentration in the top
four firms, and its geographic concentration.

Olson argues that because of the free-rider problem, a
group will be more successful in organizing if it has a
relatively small number of members, and the benefits of
its actions are unevenly spread.[13] Pincus argues that a
geographically concentrated industry should be better at
overcoming the free-rider problem due to better intra-
industry communication.[14] Brock and Magee, however,
maintain that geographically dispersed industries are
more effective politically because of the greater number
of political jurisdictions that they represent.[15]
Olson also argues that a lobbying organization is
usually not formed, or resources are not forthcoming in
large amounts, until a crisis or repeated set of crises
serve to form a common interest for the group.[16] It is
important to note that Pincus' analysis was based on

---

[13] Mancur Olson, _The Logic of Collective Action_,
(Cambridge: Harvard University Press, 1965).

[14] Jonathan J. Pincus, "Pressure Groups and the
Pattern of Tariffs," _Journal of Political Economy_,
Vol. 83, No.4, 1975, pp. 757-779.

[15] Brock and Magee, "An Economic Theory of Politics."

[16] Mancur Olson, "The Political Economy of Comparative Growth Rates," (mimeographed) 1979, as cited in
Anderson and Baldwin, "The Political Market for Protection," p.7.

antebellum tariffs; it is probably true that today geographic considerations play a much smaller role in an industry's ability to organize.

In testing industry characteristics that lead to a higher rate of protection, Anderson and Baldwin found that industry concentration was a key factor.[17] They also found that an industry is likely to receive a higher rate of protection the lower its rate of growth, the more labor intensive it is, the smaller its value-added share of output, and the lower the average wage or skill level of employees in the industry.[18]

In another study, Baldwin examines the case of the steel industry and the events leading to the introduction of the trigger price system in 1977, to illustrate the type of political and informational effort required by an industry before a President is likely to take protectionist actions on its behalf.[19] The steel industry mounted a widespread publicity campaign, including

---

[17]Anderson and Baldwin, "The Political Market for Protection," p. 14.

[18]Ibid.

[19]Robert E. Baldwin, "U.S. Political Pressures Against Adjustment to Greater Imports," in eds. Wontack Hong and Lawrence B. Krause, Trade and Growth of the Advanced Developing Countries in the Pacific Basin, (Seoul: Korea Development Institute, 1981), p.530.

appeals to the public as well as to the Government, and
as a result was able to mobilize significant support in
Congress, leading to the formation of the Steel Caucus
with an initial membership of 150 members. Baldwin
argues that because of this groundwork, when the
President moved to assist the industry, it seemed to be
because public opinion demanded it, rather than because
he was giving special treatment to a particular industry.[20] Baldwin concludes that small industries are
typically not successful with this approach because they
do not have the financial or voting power to be able to
induce a substantial number of Congressmen to pursue
their interests, and the size of their labor force is
not large enough to merit Presidential action.

Richard Caves tests three different models of the
process of political choice to see which best explain
the variation of tariff rates protecting Canada's
manufacturing industries.[21] He looks at three models:
the pressure group model, which focuses on an industries' ability to organize a pressure group; the adding
machine model, which postulates that what matters in
obtaining protection is the number of votes an industry

[20]Ibid.

[21]Richard E. Caves, "Economic Models of Political
Choice: Canada's Tariff Structure," Canadian Journal of
Economics, Vol.9, No.2, 1976, p.278.

has; and the national policy model, which postulates that the tariff structure reflects the allocation of resources and industry mix that are deemed desirable as a matter of national policy. The best performing model is the interest group model. He argues that an industry's ability to secure protection depends, in large part, on its organizational capacity relative to that of the losers, and therefore on the relative size of the gains and losses.[22]

Cheh uses the adjustment assistance model, which postulates that governments look at the ability of workers to adjust to greater import competition in making decisions on duty cuts. Explanatory variables used in this model are labor-output coefficients, percentage of unskilled workers, the age of workers, and the initial duty rate. Cheh examined U.S. tariff-reduction policy in the Kennedy Round and found that the interindustry variation in U.S. nominal tariff concessions could be partially attributed to a policy of minimizing labor adjustment costs.[23] Cheh hypothesizes that lower cuts are also expected in high duty industries, since a given percentage cut in a high duty item

---

[22]Ibid., p.287.

[23]John Cheh, "United States Concessions in the Kennedy Round and Short-Run Labor Adjustment Costs," Journal of International Economics, vol.4, 1974.

results in a greater relative reduction in the item's
import price (and thus puts more adjustment pressure on
the domestic producers) than the same percentage cut in
a low duty item.

Riedel uses Cheh's model to test whether the same was
true for West Germany.[24] West Germany, however, could
not follow an independent tariff-cutting strategy
because it was restricted to negotiate, as part of the
EEC, on the common external tariff. While Riedel's
results showed that nominal tariffs were reduced most in
those industries enjoying the highest levels of protection at the time of the negotiations, he found
evidence indicating that reductions in effective total
protection were tempered by consideration of short-run
labor adjustment problems.[25] His results suggest that,
in order to circumvent its lack of autonomy in tariff
negotiations, West Germany shifted from trade barriers
to domestic assistance to address labor adjustment
problems.

Lavergne tests three models-- the interest group model,
the labor adjustment cost model, and the status quo

---

[24]James Riedel, "Tariff Concessions in the Kennedy
Round and the Structure of Protection in West Germany,"
Journal of International Economics, vol.7, 1977.

[25]Ibid., p. 140.

model-- to see which best explains the current U.S.
tariff structure. The most powerful model was the
status quo model, which postulates that current duty
levels and recent duty cuts are positively correlated
with duty levels that existed several years ago, because
of the Government's desire to maintain the status quo of
the social welfare function.[26] He shows that despite
the substantial tariff reductions which have been made
in the last half century, the tariff levels that
prevailed under the Smoot-Hawley Act remain by far the
most important predictor of the tariff structure as it
currently stands. In his view, there are two reasons
why duty cuts are correlated with the historical level
of protection. One is the desire by Government officials to avoid large adjustment costs for an industry.
The second is the Government's desire to maintain the
status quo because of the uncertainty associated with
any large change. Corden also stresses that there is a
public goal of ensuring that certain income groups do
not incur significant income losses through a change in
the status quo.[27]

The models discussed above describe the political

---

[26]R.P. Lavergne, <u>The Political Economy of U.S.
Tariffs</u>, (New York: Academic Press, 1983), p.165.

[27]Max W. Corden, <u>Trade Policy and Economic Welfare</u>,
(London: Oxford University Press, 1974), pp.107-111.

behavior process leading to protection, and the economic characteristics of industries that tend to be successful in obtaining protection. Although it is clear that all the political and economic determinants of protectionism discussed are interrelated, the literature has not yet developed direct measures to determine the causality of protection.[28] Cheh, Baldwin, and Lavergne all cite previously existing levels of protection as a criterion to determine the level of tariff cuts in a tariff negotiation. It seems reasonable to assume that the existing tariff levels in a particular industry sector reflect underlying conditions, such as labor adjustment costs and an industry's ability to organize. But, the literature has not fully addressed some important questions. Do industries with low wages and unskilled workers have a higher motivation to organize into a political pressure group? Do large, concentrated, low wage industries succeed in obtaining protection because of their ability to organize and exert political pressure, or by virtue of a genuine economic need? Finally, does protection lead to an industry's growing inability to compete against imports, thus leading to a desire for additional protection?

---

[28]Baldwin, "Trade Policies in Developed Countries," p. 581.

It is also important to point out some technical problems with the above studies. To conclude that industries that obtain protection are low wage seems to conflict with the fact that the steel and auto industries (industries that have received protection) are high-wage industries and that sometimes high-wage industries attract imports because of their wage level. Perhaps the fact that they are high-wage industries was overridden by the fact that these industries are very large, well organized, and politically powerful. Baldwin shows that large industries are successful in obtaining relief due to their visibility, yet very small industries are often able to obtain protection precisely because of their lack of visibility. Some trade economists maintain that the escape clause has become relegated to a technical-level relief measure, reserved for small and politically weak industries, and that politically powerful industries (such as textiles, televisions, steel, and automobiles) now obtain relief through bilaterally negotiated restrictions.[29]

Several studies also neglect to mention other groups which play a role in opposing protection, such as

[29]James Riedel, "United States Trade Policy: From Multilateralism to Bilateralism?" in Free Trade in the World Economy, ed. Herbert Giersch, (Tubingen: J.C.B. Mohr (Paul Siebeck), 1987).

foreign governments, importers, and intermediary users. Although the ability of foreign governments to influence U.S. government officials is generally limited because they are not voting constituents, exceptions occur when the United States has significant foreign policy interests that take precedence over trade policy concerns. Importers and intermediary users of imported goods do play a role in opposing protection. Although in general they tend to be less well organized than producers, they are more effective than consumers. In the recent escape clause case on copper, the key groups opposing protection for copper producers were inter- mediary users of copper.

Despite these problems, all the articles confirm that industries which are successful in obtaining protection tend to have common characteristics. The economic motivation for obtaining protection is labor adjustment costs, and the political motivation is organizational pressure. Both are key factors in obtaining protection or resisting trade liberalization. Industries that already have protection as a result of either or both of these factors are successful in maintaining that protection as well as minimizing any further liberali- zation.

C. Industry Differences in Trade Negotiations

The current tariff structure in the U.S. is the result of gradual multilateral tariff liberalization. The degree of liberalization from industry to industry, however, has varied considerably. A number of studies have examined which industries are more likely to receive deeper tariff cuts in the course of a trade negotiation.

In his analysis of the impact of pressure groups on the Tokyo Round of multilateral negotiations (1973-1979), Baldwin notes that two components reflect domestic pressures shaping duty reductions in a multilateral negotiation: the ability and willingness of an industry to provide funds for lobbying efforts, and the willingness of the President and the voters to grant protection to an industry.[30] Both of these factors are important because, while the President may be willing to exempt a particular industry from duty reductions, he may not take the action if the industry does not explain its case to the him and the public.[31]

---

[30]Baldwin, "U.S. Political Pressures Against Adjustment to Greater Imports," p.530.

[31]Ibid., p.533.

Baldwin tested a series of variables to determine which
correlate best with the pattern of industries that were
successful in obtaining lower than average duty cuts in
the Tokyo Round. Characteristics such as industry
concentration and geographic concentration did not
provide significant statistical results. Two variables
that reflect the relative change in an industry's income
as a result of a duty cut were also not significant.
Changes in the industry's employment, a factor which
could shock a group into organizing to oppose trade
liberalization, was significant. Coefficients for the
average wage, the labor/valueadded ratio, and the ratio
of unskilled to skilled workers were all significant, as
was the import penetration ratio. A measure of political power, the total employment in an industry, was
also significant.

Although U.S. negotiators in the Tokyo Round had agreed
to a formula under which high duties were to be cut more
than low duties, in fact, they offered a set of cuts
that had the opposite result. Baldwin attributes this
behavior to the fact that high duty industries can be
expected to resist duty reductions more than low duty
sectors.[32] As U.S. negotiators in the Kennedy Round
argued, even a uniform, across-the-board percentage cut

---

[32]Ibid., p.546.

is likely to put more competitive pressure on high duty industries than on low duty industries.[33] Although Baldwin's results showed that characteristics such as geographic and industry concentration were not significant, his finding that the high duty sectors resisted duty cuts more than the low duty sectors seems to indicate some level of political pressure and ability to organize on the part of the high duty industries.

In his article analyzing the pattern of Congressional voting on the 1974 Trade Act, Baldwin concludes that Congressmen typically seek compromise, "second best" solutions, in order to accommodate competing interests. Congressmen faced with trade liberalizing legislation put forth by an administration of their own political persuasion, yet also faced with pressures from industries in their districts which claim injury from imports, will likely seek legislation combining protective measures for the industries in their districts and tariff-cutting authority for all other industries.[34]

---

[33]Robert E. Baldwin, "Tariff-Cutting Techniques in the Kennedy Round," in eds. R.E. Caves, H.G. Johnson, and P.B. Kennen, Trade, Growth, and the Balance of Payments, (Chicago: Rand McNally, 1965).

[34]Baldwin, "The Political Economy of Postwar U.S. Trade Policy", p. 14.

Baldwin's theory of liberal trade legislation with
individual protectionist exceptions can be extended to
trade agreements. Since trade agreements must be passed
by the Congress in order to be implemented into U.S.
law, U.S. negotiators are necessarily influenced by what
the Congress will pass. The result is liberalizing
agreements with individual protectionist exceptions,
designed to accommodate pressures on key groups of Congressmen. We have seen that certain industries are more
successful in obtaining protection and this tendency can
also be extended to the negotiation of trade agreements. While Congressmen may be able to reject most
pleas for exclusion or leniency in a tariff-cutting
agreement, they will make exceptions for industries in
their districts that are large and highly visible,
whether as a result of labor adjustment concerns,
political pressure or both.

D. The Role of Politics in Trade Policy Formation

Political scientists have tried to analyze the role of
politics in U.S. trade policy, and trade legislation in
particular. The earliest work on this topic is
Schattschneider's book, published in 1935, on the Smoot-

Hawley Tariff Bill.[35] His book, which concluded that pressure groups played a key role in determining the outcome of the 1929 Smoot-Hawley Tariff Bill, "set the tone for a whole generation of political writing on pressure groups."[36]

Almost forty years later, Bauer, Pool, and Dexter arrived at the opposite conclusion in their comprehensive study of the effect of pressure groups on trade policy and legislation between 1953-62. They argue that, "the stereotype notion of omnipotent pressure groups becomes completely untenable once there are groups aligned on both sides. The result of opposing equipotent forces is stalemate."[37] Bauer, Pool, and Dexter also dismiss the image of the venal lobbyists portrayed in Schattschneider's study and instead claim that interest groups play an important role in the American political system. They write that in articulating their grievances and interests, interest groups provide expert information to the government, and act as

---

[35]E. E. Schattschneider, Politics, Pressures, and the Tariff: A Study of Free Enterprise in Pressure Politics, as Shown in the 1929-1930 Revision of the Tariff, (New York: Prentice-Hall, Inc., 1935).

[36]Raymond Bauer, Ithiel de Sola Pool, and L.A. Dexter, American Business and Public Policy, (New York: Atherton Press, 1963), p.25.

[37]Ibid., p.398.

mutually suspicious watchdogs to sniff out each other's importunities and make these visible to Congress and the public. David Truman argues that Bauer, Pool, and Dexter's main point is that Congress and the political system do not take instructions from interest groups, rather Congressmen act as independent agents, using information from interest groups to make their own decisions.[38]

Robert Pastor, in his study, <u>Congress and the Politics of U.S. Foreign Economic Policy 1929-1976</u>, takes a different approach.[39] He contends that since Smoot-Hawley Congress has been moving to increasingly liberalize trade and reduce barriers. Pastor argues that in the eighteenth and nineteenth centuries, legislators represented sections of the country rather than constituents. These sectionalist groups coalesced within particular parties so that Republicans became the party of high tariffs and big business, and Democrats the party of low tariffs. Smoot-Hawley represented the culmination of these developments-- interest groups were rampant, Presidential leadership was nonexistent, and

---

[38]David B. Truman, <u>The Governmental Process</u>, (New York: Alfred Knopf, 1971). p. 33.

[39]Robert A. Pastor, <u>Congress and the Politics of U.S. Foreign Economic Policy 1929-1976</u>, (Los Angeles: University of California Press, 1980).

Congress raised tariffs to their highest point in the
twentieth century.

Pastor claims that the Reciprocal Trade Agreements Act
of 1934 represents the real watershed in U.S. trade
policy history. It was the first time that Congress did
not debate individual tariffs; instead it formally
delegated tariffmaking authority to the President which
allowed him to begin negotiations with other countries
to reduce tariffs. According to Pastor, from 1934 on
interest groups were organized on the sector level and
lined up on both sides of the issue, cancelling out
specific influence in all but two kinds of cases. When
industry-specific interest groups had a complaint, they
forced the Congress to address it on a general level,
for example by changing the laws on adjustment assistance or countervailing duties. For those industries
like steel or textiles which were clearly national in
scope, specific pressures forced the President to define
an industrial policy for these sectors and negotiate
this policy internationally.[40]

Pastor further argues that the Congress continues to be
free trade oriented and allegations that it is unduly
influenced by interest groups stems from a misunder-

[40]Ibid., p.189.

standing of the Congressional process. Despite the fact that legislators often introduce protectionist bills and amendments, the legislation that is passed is liberal. He calls this the "cry and sigh" paradox of U.S. trade policy.[41] A legislator introduces a bill to send signals to different groups-- to ailing industries in his district that he is trying to do something, to foreign governments that he is concerned about import competition, and to his own government to push them to negotiate more aggressively. The introduction of such a bill leads to accommodation by the Administration and foreign governments, and in turn congressional frustration drops and a liberal trade bill is passed.

These analyses of the role of pressure groups on trade legislation leave important issues unaddressed. While Schattschneider's study may overestimate the power of interest groups, Bauer, Pool, and Dexter fail to question why some industries get special treatment and exceptions in trade legislation, while others do not. Their assertion that all interest groups have "equipotent" opponents is not supported by the economic evidence cited earlier in the chapter that some industries are better able to obtain protection than others.

---

[41]Ibid., p.191.

Although Pastor offers a more convincing analysis of the Congressional approach to trade policy than either Schattschneider or Bauer, Pool and Dexter, he does not provide a complete picture. While no one would argue that tariffs have been significantly liberalized since SmootHawley, it is equally obvious that important sectoral exceptions to that liberalization exist. While Pastor acknowledges that steel and textiles constitute exceptions to the rule of interest groups cancelling each other out, he also makes the questionable assertion that these cases are not significant in the broad liberalizing trend of U.S. trade policy.

The role of the Executive branch in trade policy, and the interaction between the Executive branch and Congress are both neglected in the above studies. Baldwin argues that the President has historically been more liberal on trade policy than Congress because his responsibility for foreign policy leads to a reluctance to take protectionist actions that may antagonize trading partners.[42] The President is also less vulnerable at election time to the local constituent pressures that face a Congressman. At the same time, it is very difficult for a President to resist granting

---

[42]Robert E. Baldwin, The Political Economy of U.S. Import Policy, (Cambridge: Massachussettes Institute of Technology Press, 1985), p. 121.

protection to industries that are significant in providing votes, since major industries such as textiles, autos, and steel have the resources necessary to apply political pressure on both Congress and the Executive branch.[43]

Within the Executive branch, policies are often made by civil servants, who are not directly responsible to the voters. Baldwin contends that workers in government agencies try to promote the interests of the agencies' constituencies.[44] Personal contacts with representatives from the groups that agencies represent reinforce this favorable attitude of government agencies. For example, civil servants from the Department of Labor deal with labor representatives, civil servants from the Department of Commerce deal with business executives, and civil servants from the Department of Agriculture deal with domestic farmers. Nonelected government officials thus gain on-the-job knowledge about the economic problems of the groups they address, but learn little about difficulties faced by other groups. Other researchers have suggested that civil servants adopt these attitudes because they are more likely to succeed in the job and achieve the kind of cooperation they need

[43]Ibid., p.122.

[44]Ibid., p. 126.

work effectively. Both Stigler and Peltzman have argued
that the net effect of these various factors is that
civil servants at all levels in various government
agencies tend to adopt the economic and social view-
points of the groups they serve.[45]

The tendency of government employees to be concerned
about the economic conditions of the populations they
represent raises the importance of personal contact for
industries interested in obtaining protection, and the
issue of lobbying the Executive branch as well as the
legislative. Baldwin states that industries that
possess the resources necessary to touch base frequently
with civil servants in relevant agencies and to provide
them with substantive analysis of their problems are
more likely to obtain help.[46]

In the years following Pastor's 1980 book, a general
consensus has formed that trade policy has become more
protectionist. Baldwin claims that the delegation of
authority over trade from Congress to the President in

---

[45]"Toward a More General Theory of Regulation,"
S. Peltzman, Journal of Law and Economics, vol.19, 1976,
pp. 211-248, and George J. Stigler, "The Economic Theory
of Regulation," in The Citizen and the State, (Chicago:
The University of Chicago Press, 1975).

[46]Baldwin, The Political Economy of Import Policy,
p. 128.

the late 1930s was an important prerequisite to the creation of a liberal trade system because it reduced the ability of pressure groups to influence trade policy. Over time, however, Congress has incrementally tried to recoup lost power and narrow the President's discretionary authority over trade policy. Riedel postulates that this shift has contributed to the increased success of special interests at lobbying for protection.[47]

Jan Tumlir views the transfer of authority over trade policy from Congress to the President as the fundamental source of instability in U.S. trade policy, and part of the increasing power of the Executive branch over economic regulation in general.[48] He argues that the Executive branch is as susceptible to influence from pressure groups as Congress. In fact, he notes that in the Executive branch, special interests can be accommodated without the constraint of having to build coalitions and win a majority vote as in the Congress, and without the benefit of public discussion.

Economists like Tumlir and Riedel have argued that the

---

[47]Riedel, "United States Trade Policy," p. 98.

[48]Jan Tumlir, Protectionism: Trade Policy in Democratic Societies, (Washington D.C.: American Enterprise Institute, 1985), p.14.

changes in the domestic trade policy process have caused
an increase in discriminatory protection--bilateral,
sectorspecific import restrictions such as exist in
textiles, steel, and automobiles. Pastor pointed to the
"cry and sigh" paradox as an affirmation of the liberal
trade orientation of Congress. Perhaps, however, the
point is that by introducing protectionist legislation,
the Congress can often achieve whatever protection it
wants through nonlegislative means. That liberal
legislation is passed is not necessarily an indication
that Congress has not provided protection to certain
pressure groups.

A recent example is the case of automobile imports from
Japan. Because the U.S. auto industry is highly
visible, it was successful in obtaining a significant
amount of support in the Congress. Numerous bills that
would have required imported automobiles to have a
certain percent of U.S. content were introduced into the
Congress. Although none of these protectionist bills
passed, as Pastor would predict, their existence pushed
the Administration into negotiating a voluntary restraint agreement with Japan on automobile imports into
the U.S. Thus, while protectionist bills may not turn
into protectionist legislation, they may nonetheless
result in protectionist trade policy. The auto case is

a particularly good example because it illustrates once again the special treatment available to politically powerful industries.

Tumlir argues that it is not the increased role of Congress that has caused this protectionist shift, but rather the "good cop--bad cop" routine used by the two branches of government. In his view, Congress plays the "bad cop" with its threats of protectionist legislation, and the administration plays the "good cop," using these threats to its advantage to negotiate bilateral import restraints.[49] According to Riedel, a greater problem in the shift toward protection is that pressure groups now lobby the Executive branch more intensively because government bureaucrats have more control than before over certain trade decisions (such as when to impose a quota under the Multifiber Agreement).[50] Moreover, these dealings are far less transparent than dealings with Congress. While civil servants are lobbied regarding decisions they control, those decisions are limited. The majority of trade authority still rests with the Congress, and to the extent that the Executive branch is responsive to pressure group concerns, it is because it knows that it must craft trade policies or negotiate

---

[49]Ibid., p.39.

[50]Riedel, "United States Trade Policy," p.99.

trade agreements that Congress will approve.

E. Developing a Framework

The studies discussed in this chapter have utilized a
broad range of analytical approaches. Taken as a whole
they provide a useful framework for analyzing the
political economy of trade negotiations and agreements.
The economic research demonstrates that pressure groups
play a role in trade policy formation because producers
are well informed about their gains from protection, and
consumers are less informed about their losses. Because
producers are better informed and better able to organize, they are also better able to influence the votes
of government officials than are consumers.

All the studies confirm that the industries that are
successful in obtaining protection tend to be large,
concentrated, laborintensive, with low average wages and
high import penetration. These industries are also able
to organize their members and interests. Thus, industries are successful at obtaining protection or resisting liberalization as a result of economic considerations such as labor adjustment costs and political
pressure from interest groups. Industries that already
have high tariffs, as a result of either or both of

these, are successful in maintaining that protection, and minimizing trade liberalization. Since trade agreements must be passed by the Congress in order to be implemented into U.S. law, U.S. negotiators are necessarily influenced by what the Congress will pass. The result is liberalizing agreements with individual protectionist exceptions, designed to accommodate pressures on key groups of Congressmen.

Several of the studies discussed postulated that duty cuts are correlated with the historical level of protection because of the government's desire to avoid large adjustment costs for any industry and to protect certain income groups from incurring significant income losses.[51] Whatever the original reasons for protection, once an industry is protected, it is politically difficult to reduce that protection. Congress is driven by constituent concerns to maintain that protection, and bureaucrats reinforce these trends, partly through an attempt to meet the wishes of Congress, and partly through their own over-familiarity with the industry.

Tumlir's argument that Congress plays the "bad cop" with

---

[51]Corden, Trade Policy and Economic Welfare, pp.107-111.

its threats of protection and that the administration
uses this to its advantage to negotiate bilateral import
restraints can also be carried over to the negotiation
of trade agreements. Because of the necessary partnership between the two branches of government, they
usually work closely together to craft a piece of legislation or trade agreement that both can live with and
sell to their respective constituencies and interests.
Thus, the art of negotiating a trade agreement is one of
giving the negotiating partner the perception that it
has obtained enough concessions to make the agreement
worthwhile (this usually means increased access to the
U.S. market), and at the same time giving the domestic
constituency and the Congress the perception that
certain politically sensitive industries will continue
to be protected.

The above findings are useful in developing a framework
for analyzing the U.S.-Israel FTA negotiations. In
discussing the events that led up to the decision to
negotiate the FTA and the actual negotiation, this study
will examine the influences brought to bear on U.S
negotiators to negotiate an agreement that Congress
would approve; the interaction of Congress and the
Executive branch in the course of the negotiation with
Congress often acting as the "bad cop"; the role of

interest groups in the negotiation process and in particular the pressure to continue protecting industries that are already heavily protected; and finally, how these pressures resulted in a free trade area agreement that sought to liberalize bilateral trade completely, and resulted in an agreement that maintained significant barriers to trade.

II. Economic Framework of the FTA

In order to assess the FTA negotiation process it is important to understand the economic framework within which it took place. This chapter starts by examining the bilateral trading relationship between the U.S. and Israel, including the barriers to trade that existed prior to the negotiation of the FTA. The second section of the chapter describes the provisions and limitations of the free trade area agreement that both countries entered into on September 1, 1985. To analyze the potential effect of the FTA, the third section of the chapter briefly reviews the economic theory of free trade areas, examines the projected economic impact of the U.S.Israel FTA, and concludes with a discussion of the potential costs and benefits of the agreement to both countries.

A. Trade Overview

In recent years, the United States has been Israel's single largest trading partner, providing a market for approximately 25% of Israel's exports and supplying about 20% of its nonmilitary imports. In contrast, Israel ranked 34th in terms of U.S. import suppliers, making up only 0.5% of total U.S. imports in 1983. In the years prior to the FTA, the U.S. had a consistent trade surplus with Israel. In 1983, prior to the negotiation of the FTA, the U.S. had a bilateral trade surplus of $465 million in its trade with Israel. In that year, U.S. imports from Israel were $1.25 billion, and U.S. exports to Israel were $1.72 billion. Although the U.S. is Israel's largest individual market, a majority of Israel's trade is with the European Economic Community (EEC). The U.S.- Israel FTA is the first free trade area for the U.S., and the second for Israel, which has a less comprehensive free trade area with the EEC. The 1975 Israel-EEC Preferential Agreement eliminates tariff barriers on trade in manufactured goods between the two entities. Under the terms of this agreement, imports of manufactured products from Israel were granted duty-free entry to the EEC in July 1977, except for certain products considered to be import-sensitive by the EEC on which full duty elimination was delayed until December 1979. Israel eliminated duties on about 60% of its manufactured imports from the EEC in January 1980, and complete duty-free treatment will be phased in by January 1989. The Israel-EEC Preferential Agreement also attempted to provide for a substantial reduction in barriers to trade in agricultural pro-ducts. Although the EEC agreed to make tariff reduc-tions on about 80% of its agricultural imports from

Israel, due to the limits imposed by the EEC's Common Agricultural Policy (CAP), Israeli exporters were still required to comply with the CAP's nontariff requirements and are often faced with quotas and voluntary export restraint agreements. As a result, reciprocal Israeli agricultural tariff concessions to the EEC have been very limited.

Table 1 gives the history of Israeli imports from and exports to the United States and the EEC. Looking at the pattern of trade, we see that Israel's imports and exports decreased between 1980 and 1983. During this period, Israel's exchange rate did not devalue at the same rate as its inflation increased, resulting in a depreciation in Israel's real exchange rate and a decline in competitiveness. Bruno and Fischer[1] write that after Israel's financial liberalization in 1977, its economy moved into a period of runaway inflation, rising from 25% in 1977 to almost 400% in 1984. A second factor in the decline of Israel's net exports is the return of the Sinai oil fields to Egypt in 1979, in

---

[1]Michael Bruno and Stanley Fischer, "The Infla-tionary Process: Shocks and Accommodation," in ed. Yoram Ben-Porath, The Israeli Economy: Maturing through Crises, (Cambridge: Harvard University Press, 1986).

accordance with the Camp David Peace Treaty,[2] causing a
large jump in oil imports. Looking at Table 1 this jump
can be calculated as the $1.5 billion increase in
Israel's imports from the rest of the world (primarily
the oil-exporting nations). During that period, imports
from the rest of the world grew from 24% to 34% as a
percent of overall Israeli imports. Looking at Israel's
non-oil imports during that time we see that Israel's
imports from the U.S. fell and imports from the EEC
increased slightly as a percentage of non-oil imports.

An analysis of Israel's exports reveals that since 1975
the U.S. has been steadily growing in importance as an
export market for Israel. Between 1980 and 1982, there
was a drop of six percentage points in exports to the
EEC, and an increase of four percentage points in
exports to the U.S. and two percentage points in exports
to the rest of the world. Although Israel's exports to
the EEC increased slightly in 1983, exports to the
U.S. continued to increase as well, with exports to the
rest of the world falling. Under the terms of Israel's
free trade area with the EEC, EEC duty-free treatment of
manufactured imports from Israel was phased in by the
end of 1979. Table 1, however, does not seem to

---

[2]Israeli figures showed that total oil imports
jumped from $1075.7 million in 1975 to $2,470.2 million
in 1980, in constant dollars.

TABLE 1

HISTORY OF ISRAEL'S EXPORTS AND IMPORTS[3]

Israel's total exports (millions of $)	% to EEC	% to U.S.	% to ROW
1970	1,854.0	39.97	21.34	38.60
1975	3,600.5	38.80	17.56	43.62
1980	6,461.5	39.42	18.30	42.23
1982	5,255.3	33.26	22.05	44.63
1983	4,924.6	34.30	26.89	38.79

Israel's total imports	% from EEC	% from U.S.	% from ROW
1970	3,480.9	59.78	22.18	18.03
1975	7,036.4	51.31	24.00	24.66
1980	9,366.4	46.04	19.30	34.65
1982	8,116.1	47.48	18.99	33.50
1983	8,273.0	52.15	19.21	28.64

Israel's non-oil imports	% from EEC	% from U.S.	% from ROW
1975	5,960.7	60.57	28.33	11.10
1980	6,896.6	62.53	19.25	18.22
1982	6,256.1	61.60	24.64	13.76
1983	6,832.5	63.14	23.26	13.60

Source: Statistical Abstract of Israel.

---

[3]Trade figures were converted from Israeli shekels to constant 1982 dollars.

indicate shifts in Israel's exports resulting from duty elimination by the EEC. Since the EEC has preferential agreements allowing duty-free access with a large number of other countries, including almost all of its former colonies,[4] it is possible that Israel's FTA with the EEC offers Israel minimal real export advantages. Furthermore, with the accession of Greece, Spain, and Portugal to the EEC, many of Israel's traditional exports to the EEC, such as olives and citrus, are less competitive.

On the import side, Israel eliminated 60% of its duties on manufactured imports from the EEC in 1980 and will phase in duty-free treatment by 1989. Israel's non-oil imports from the EEC, as a proportion of total non-oil imports, increased slightly from 1975 to 1983. This increase is most likely the result of Israel's phasing in of duty elimination to the EEC. Israel's imports from the U.S., as a percent of non-oil imports, declined between 1975 and 1980 and have risen slowly since then.

---

[4]The EEC has a preference agreement with the countries of the European Free Trade Association (EFTA). It had a preference agreement with Greece, Spain, and Portugal until their accession into the Common Market. It also has preference agreements with the Maghreb countries (Algeria, Tunisia, and Morocco), the Mashrek countries (Egypt, Jordan, Lebanon, and Syria), Cyprus, Israel, Malta, and Turkey, the ACP-EEC Convention of Lome (59 African Countries) and the OCT-EEC Convention (the Pacific countries and terrritories that are or were colonies of France, the U.K, and the Netherlands).

There does not, however, seem to be evidence suggesting significant trade diversion from the United States as a result of Israel's free trade agreement with the EEC.

Tariff Barriers

In 1983, 93.1% of U.S. imports from Israel entered duty-free,[5] 55.2% entered duty-free on a most-favored-nation (MFN)[6] basis, and 37.9% entered duty-free under the U.S. Generalized System of Preferences (GSP).[7] Of the total Israeli exports to the United States in 1983, only 6.9% or $83.2 million were dutiable. Table 2 traces the history of U.S. imports from Israel from 1978 to 1985, while Table 3 lists Israel's top exports to the United States, in terms of dollar value, by product and tariff classification. Table 2 reveals a sharp drop in dutiable imports from Israel between 1980 and 1981, and

---

[5]U.S. Department of Commerce, Import Monthly, series 145, Washington D.C., 1983. Statistics are based on dollar value.

[6] The MFN principle states that all nations that are signatories to the General Agreement on Tariffs and Trade are all "most-favored-nations" and must therefore all receive the same tariff treatment.

[7]GSP is a temporary program of unilateral duty-free tariff preferences that the United States offers to all eligible developing countries. The program was enacted into law in 1974, and has been periodically renewed and amended since that time. See Appendix I to this chapter for a detailed discussion of the provisions of and amendments to the GSP program.

TABLE 2

U.S. IMPORTS FROM ISRAEL BY DUTY STATUS[8]

	Total imports	GSP-free imports	MFN-free imports	Dutiable imports
	(millions of dollars)			
1978	992.9	265.9	125.9	601.1
1979	951.1	359.9	121.1	469.7
1980	1098.0	262.2	255.2	580.6
1981	1313.7	345.2	887.5	80.9
1982	1162.1	403.5	678.4	80.2
1983	1204.4	456.6	664.4	83.2
1984	1616.5	660.0	844.7	110.8
1985*	1897.7	*	*	*

Source: U.S. Department of Commerce, Import Weekly, series 145, Washington D.C.

*The FTA entered into effect in September 1985.

---

[8]Trade figures are in constant 1982 dollars.

TABLE 3

LEADING U.S. IMPORTS FROM ISRAEL BY TARIFF CLASSIFICATION
(ranked by 1983 trade value)

Leading MFN duty-free imports TSUSA category (5-digit categories)	Trade value (Thousand U.S. dollars)	U.S. duty rate (1983 % rates)
52032 Diamonds under 1/2 carat	342,253	0
52033 Diamonds over 1/2 carat	152,145	0
48050 Potassium Chloride	41,431	0
69441 Aircraft, nonmilitary	37,964	0
52038 Emeralds	17,857	0
Leading GSP duty-free imports TSUSA category		
74014 Jewelry of precious metals	47,773	9.3
70963 X-ray apparatus	45,041	2.3
74013 Gold necklaces*	41,218	9.3
77251 Telephonic apparatus	34,172	8.5
70917 Electro-medical apparatus parts	16,246	5.1
Leading dutiable imports TSUSA category		
4166 Processed tomato products	11,139	14.7
4165 Tomato sauce	9,504	13.6
8610 Resistor parts	4,833	6.0
8384 Women's & girl's swim suits	3,938	22.4
6624 Cotton towels	3,403	11.7

*In 1981, the tariff item 74010 was disaggregated to items 74013 (gold necklaces) and 74014 (jewelry of precious metals except gold). This division preserved Israel's access to the GSP program in this commodity. Without it, Israel's exports of gold necklaces would have exceeded the competitive needs limit in 1980.

Source: Office of the U.S. Trade Representative, unpublished trade statistics.

imports into the U.S. rose starting in 1980 because of
the phasing in of the duty reductions resulting from the
Tokyo Round of Multilateral Trade Negotiations (MTN)
concluded in 1979. The sharp drop in dutiable imports
from Israel is almost entirely accounted for by the
elimination of duties on diamonds as part of the MTN
tariff elimination. Nearly $500 million worth of
diamonds imports from Israel went from being dutied at
between 1 and 2 percent to being duty-free under MFN in
1981.

At the time of the FTA negotiations, Israel was the
seventh largest beneficiary of duty-free treatment under
the GSP program, receiving 4.4% of the total GSP
benefits offered by the United States, in terms of
dollar value. Between 1976 and 1983, Israel increased
its use of the GSP program, with GSP exports growing, as
a share of total exports to the United States, from
27.4% in 1976 to 37.9% in 1983, in terms of dollar
value. Israel also used the GSP program to diversify
its exports to the U.S. As an indication of this
diversification, the percent of Israel's exports to the
U.S. that benefitted from GSP, in terms of the number of
tariff items under GSP, increased from 17.3% to 26.3%
over the 1976-83 period. Likewise, the share of
Israel's top ten exports entering the U.S. duty-free

under GSP as a share of its total GSP duty-free exports, declined from 65.2% in 1976 to 50.6% in 1983.

In contrast to the low tariff barriers faced by Israel in exporting to the United States, U.S. exports to Israel faced higher tariffs on a larger proportion of its goods. Sixtyone percent of U.S. exports to Israel before the FTA entered dutyfree. In addition, before the FTA, U.S. exports to Israel had tariffs averaging about 10%, while Israeli exports to the U.S. had tariffs averaging 6.1%.[9]

Nontariff Barriers

Although Israel does not face substantial tariff barriers in exporting to the U.S., it does face some serious nontariff barriers. The U.S. has significant nontariff barriers in two sectors, textiles and agriculture. The U.S. maintains a complex array of quotas and nontariff barriers governing trade in textiles under the authority of Section 204 of the Agricultural Act of 1956, and in conformity with the GATT Arrangement Regarding International Trade in Textiles, commonly

---

[9]Doral Cooper, "Free Trade Areas: New Opportunities, New Risks," Interview in International Business Review, March 1984. According to USTR records, the (unweighted) average tariff on U.S. goods was 6.1% in 1979 and was reduced to 4.2% in 1987 as the last of the Tokyo Round of tariff reductions were implemented.

referred to as the Multifiber Arrangement. Section 22
of the Agricultural Adjustment Act of 1933 authorizes
the President to impose quotas on certain agricultural
items. At the present time, import controls are in
place to protect cotton, peanuts, sugar, cheeses, and
certain other dairy products.

The U.S. also maintains a very comprehensive system of
administrative procedures regarding imports. These
administrative procedures are often regarded as nontariff barriers by U.S. trading partners. These laws
include the antidumping and countervailing duty laws
which are aimed at imports which, according to U.S. law,
are being subsidized or sold at "less than fair value,"
and two broader unfair trade regulations (Section 337 of
the Tariff Act of 1930 and section 301 of the Trade Act
of 1974). Also included is Section 201 of the Trade Act
of 1974 (the escape clause), which allows the President
to grant protection to a domestic industry that is being
injured by imports.

Israel has even more extensive nontariff barriers than
the United States. As a newly industrialized country,
Israel's government has historically been very involved
in the economy. Israel has a array of export subsidies,
protection for infant industries, and stringent per-

formance requirements as a condition for investment. In the past, Israel has also frequently resorted to the use of quantitative measures for balance of payments purposes. In addition, U.S. exports to Israel are in general subject to a variety of nontariff barriers, including a purchase tax, compulsory surcharges, unlinked deposits, excise duties, and a value-added tax on all imported products. All of these taxes are designed to regulate domestic demand as well as raise revenue.

The most important nontariff barrier is a "hidden tariff" created by the administration of the Israeli Purchasing Tax system on all imports to Israel. This hidden tariff, which as a domestic tax will not be eliminated by the FTA, may well be the largest barrier to U.S. exports. For the purposes of the purchasing tax, the taxable value of an imported product must reflect the price of domestic Israeli wholesale products. Where there is no Israeli counterpart to the imported product, the Israeli government must impute the taxable value of the import by multiplying the import price (including duties) by some factor which reflects the difference between the foreign price and the domestic wholesale price of some comparable product. This inflated import price is then used to calculate the purchasing tax,

creating the "hidden tariff." This system is known by
its Hebrew acronym-TAMA.

Summary

Prior to the negotiation of the FTA, the United States
was a large and growing export market for Israel, with
less than ten percent of those exports dutiable at relatively low rates. Israel's degree of duty-free access
to the U.S. market was, in part, the result of the fact
that Israel made very effective use of the temporary
duty-free access that it enjoyed under the GSP program.
Israel was a relatively small market for U.S. exports,
with a significant percentage of those exports dutiable
at a relatively high rate. Both countries had numerous
nontariff barriers that were more significant impedi-
ments to trade than the tariff barriers. This was the
environment in which the U.S. and Israel negotiated
their free trade area agreement.

B. The Free Trade Area Agreement

The FTA between the United States and Israel provides for the ultimate elimination of all tariffs on all goods (manufactured as well as agricultural goods) by both countries. The FTA also reduces nontariff barriers (for instance, subsidies and import licensing) and has a provision covering trade in services. All commercial trade between the U.S. and Israel will be covered by the Agreement, and all duties will be eliminated over a ten-year period, by January 1, 1995.[10] This will be accomplished in four phases:

1) Duties on items in the first tranche were eliminated immediately upon the agreement's entry into force (12/1/85). For both the U.S. and Israel the majority of products in this tranche are items with very low tariffs, no trade, or items which are already entering duty-free under GSP.

2) Duties on items in the second tranche will be eliminated, in three duty cuts, by 1/1/89. Most of the U.S. product categories in this tranche were undergoing tariff reduction or elimination as part of U.S. commitments under the Tokyo Round of GATT

---

[10]In analyzing the agreement in this study, 1982 trade data is used. This year was chosen as the base year for the FTA negotiations and was the only year for which disaggregated trade data, including tariffs was made available by the Israeli Government.

negotiations.[11] Most of Israel's product categories in this tranche will be duty-free to the EEC
by 1/1/89 as part of the Israel-EEC Preferential
Agreement.

3) Duties on items in the third tranche will have
tariffs gradually eliminated, in eight duty cuts,
over ten years. The large majority of U.S. product
categories in this tranche are textile and apparel
products. On Israel's side, items in this tranche
include textiles, batteries, generators, and
telephone equipment.

4) Duties on items in the fourth tranche will have
tariffs frozen at their current levels for five
years, at which time the United States and Israel
will agree on a schedule of tariff elimination.
Tariffs on items on this category will be completely eliminated by 1/1/95.[12] This tranche is
composed of those products each country considered
the most sensitive in terms of the agreement.
Items on the Israeli list include radio and
telephone equipment, chemical products, paper
products, passenger cars, refrigerators, tobacco
and a number of agricultural products. For the

---

[11]The MTN tariff reductions were completed on
January 1, 1987.

[12]See Appendix II for a detailed description of the
FTA agreement and its tariff and nontariff provisions.

United States, the list includes the products
identified as sensitive by the U.S. International
Trade Commission,[13] including processed tomato
products, citrus fruit juices, cut roses, olives,
and gold chains. Table 4 summarizes the breakdown
of trade in each tranche.

The nontariff portion of the agreement seeks to eliminate or reduce some of the key nontariff barriers to
trade between the United States and Israel. The
agreement is the first of its kind to recognize the
importance of reducing barriers to trade in services and
to include a separate Declaration on Services. In the
case of export subsidies, the U.S. requested that Israel
bring its practices into compliance with the GATT
Subsidies Code as part of the FTA. Israel agreed to
eliminate, over a period of six years, certain export
subsidies[14] on industrial and processed agricultural
goods in order to meet with the requirements of the
Subsidies Code.

---

[13]For a discussion of the products on the ITC list
see chapter IV, section D.

[14]The export subsidies listed in Annex 4 of the
U.S.Israel FTA specifies that elimination of the
following four subsidy programs will bring Israel into
compliance with the GATT Subsidies Code: 1) export
shipment fund, 2) export production fund, 3) imports for
exports fund, and 4) medium term capital goods export
credits.

TABLE 4

TRADE LEVELS IN EACH TRANCHE OF THE U.S.- ISRAEL FTA
(1982 trade statistics)[15]

Tranches	Amount of trade in each tranche	
	U.S. imports from Israel	Israel's imports from the U.S.
First Tranche (immediate duty elimination)	$414.7 million 80.4% of U.S. imports from Israel	$670.8 million 52.5% of Israel's imports from U.S.
Second Tranche (duty elim. by 1/1/89)	$27.8 million 5.4% of U.S. imports from Israel	$402.8 million 31.5% of Israel's imports from U.S.
Third Tranche (gradual duty elim. by 1/1/95)	$4.7 million 0.9% of U.S. imports from Israel	$39.5 million 3.0% of Israel's imports from U.S.
Fourth Tranche (five year freeze then duty elim. by 1/1/95)	$67.9 million 13.6% of U.S. imports from Israel	$164.4 million 12.8% of Israel's imports from U.S.

Source: Office of the U.S. Trade Representative, "Summary of the U.S.-Israel Free Trade Area Agreement," unpublished paper, Washington D.C., September 1985.

---

[15]It is important to note that the statistics in this table do not include the 55% of Israel's exports to the U.S. that entered the U.S. duty free under MFN since these items were not part of the negotiation.

Other nontariff provisions of the FTA go further than
the international standards set in the GATT. The
agreement restricts Israel's right to apply protective
measures which would benefit infant industries, rights
granted under GATT Article XVIII, Section C. The agreement limits Israel's rights which it would have under
the GATT to use quantitative measures for balance of
payments purposes. The FTA prohibits the use of
performance requirements as a condition for investment[16]
and provides for import licensing procedures that are
more restrictive than those contained in the GATT Code
on Import Licensing Procedures. Both countries agreed
to liberalize government procurement regulations on a
bilateral basis to a greater degree than is specified in
the Government Procurement Code.

The FTA also allows each country to maintain certain
nontariff barriers. Article 6 provides that both
nations may maintain import restrictions based on
agricultural policy considerations. Both countries have
quotas on agricultural products that will not be
affected by the FTA. Article 8 provides Israel with a
right to impose import restrictions for the purposes of
its Kosher laws. The FTA specifically addresses the

---

[16]Performance requirements are not directly
addressed in the GATT or any of its codes.

issue of escape clause safeguards and allows each party
to grant import relief to a domestic industry seriously
injured from imports.

Other nontariff barriers, however, are not covered by
that the agreement. Because the agreement does not
supercede other provisions in U.S. domestic law, all the
import relief provisions in U.S. trade law remain in
effect. Thus, the U.S. government's anti-dumping,
countervailing duty, and unfair trade regulations
(Section 337 of the Tariff Act of 1930 and Section 301
of the Trade Act of 1974) are not modified with regard
to Israel. In addition, the Multifiber Arrangement,
with its array of quotas and nontariff barriers governing textiles is not affected by the FTA.[17] Although
Israeli textile exports to the United States have
significant tariff advantages, they are still subject to
the same nontariff barriers as other textile exporters
to the U.S. On the Israeli side, the agreement does not
address the panoply of other taxes that are imposed, including a purchase tax, compulsory surcharges, unlinked
deposits, excise duties, and a value-added tax on all
imported products. Since most of these charges are re-
bated to exporters, the brunt of the charges are born by

_____

[17]For an indepth discussion of the negotiations on
textiles that took place as part U.S.-Israel FTA
negotiations, see Chapter V section C.

imports into Israel.

C. Analyzing the Effect of the U.S.- Israel FTA

This section reviews the economic theory of free trade areas in order to analyze the costs and benefits accruing to both the U.S. and Israel as a result of the FTA. Because of the analytical difficulties involved in analyzing the dynamic effects of trade integration,[18] this section will only seek to do a comparative static analysis of the FTA.[19]

Theoretical Issues

In examining the impact of the FTA the central question is how the volume and composition of bilateral trade between the U.S. and Israel will change, and how these changes will affect each country's domestic economic situation. The economic literature has analyzed the impact of entering into a free trade area in terms of the resulting changes in the volume and pattern of trade, and the net welfare effects of those changes.

---

[18]Paul Robson, The Economics of International Integration, (London: Policy Studies Institute, 1984). p.32.

[19]This analysis will only deal with the direct effects of the FTA, i.e., the reallocation of production and consumption due to price changes, assuming that production techniques, tastes, and factor supplies are unchanged.

There are two trade effects, trade creation and trade
diversion, that result from the elimination of tariffs
on exports from a trading partner in the context of the
formation of a customs union or free trade area.[20]
When a country eliminates a tariff, trade creation
generally results; however, the net domestic welfare
effect depends on whether trade diversion also occurs
and whether the welfare effects of trade creation are
greater than trade diversion. Figures 1 and 2 show how
these two effects occur when countries A and B form a
free trade area.

The best way to illustrate trade creation and diversion
is to ignore domestic production, and let D_{im} represent
the excess demand for product "x." In Figure 1, country
A imports product "x" from country B, the most efficient
producer. When A eliminates its tariff on imports from
B, A's imports from B expand. This is trade creation.
We assume here that B's supply curve of "x" is perfectly
elastic. Before the formation of the free trade area,
B's supply curve was a $(1+t)P_B$, and A purchased Q_1.
After A's elimination of its tariff to B, B's supply
curve becomes P_B, causing A's imports to expand to Q_2.

---

[20]See for example, Robson, The Economics of
International Integration, chapters 2-4.

WELFARE EFFECTS OF A FREE TRADE AREA

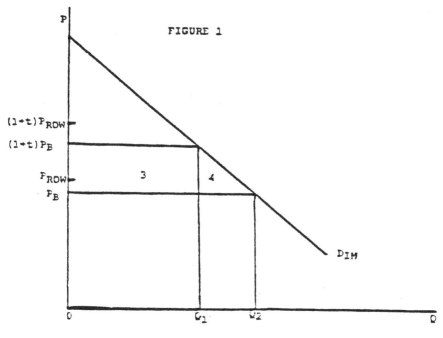

FIGURE 1

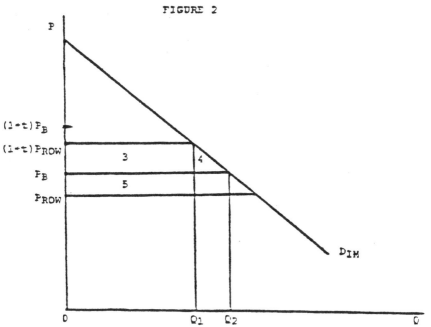

FIGURE 2

If country B is not the most efficient producer of "x,"
and A has been importing "x" more cheaply from the rest
of the world, trade diversion will occur when A and B
form a free trade area. When A eliminates its tariffs
to B, B can undercut the rest of the world, forcing A to
divert its imports of "x" to B, the less efficient
producer. Figure 2 shows that before the formation of
the free trade area, country A would import Q_1 of "x"
from the rest of the world at $(1+t)P_{row}$. After eliminating tariffs to B, A will import Q_2 of "x" from B at
P_B.

Examining the domestic welfare effects resulting from
these shifts in trade, we see in Figure 1 that when
country A enters into the free trade area with B, areas
3 and 4 represent a gain in consumer surplus by A's
consumer's of "x."[21] Area 3, however, is not a net gain
since it represents tariff revenue foregone. Thus, area
4 represents the net welfare gain to A.

Looking at the welfare effects in Figure 2, we note that
areas 3+4 again comprise a gain in consumer surplus.
Once again, area 3 represents tariff revenue foregone

[21]For a discussion on the welfare analysis resulting from a tariff elimination, see Robert E. Baldwin,
John H. Mutti and J. David Richardson, "Welfare Effects
on the United States of a Significant Tariff Reduction,"
Journal of International Economics, vol. 10, 1980.

and area 4 is a welfare gain for A. Before the free trade area, areas 3+5 measured the total tariff revenue. While area 3 is offset by a gain in consumer surplus, area 5 is paid by A's consumer's to the higher cost producers in country B, and is a pure social loss for A. If area 5 is larger than area 4, a net welfare loss occurs from the formation of a customs area.[22]

Figures 1 and 2 illustrate the impact on trade and welfare in two cases. Case 1 may apply in some industries while case 2 may apply in others. The net welfare effect of entering into a free trade area may be positive in some industries and negative in other industries. If the positive welfare effects of trade creation are greater than the negative welfare effects of trade diversion, net welfare improvement will result for a country entering a free trade area.

The above approach examines the comparative static effects of entering into a free trade area. In the longer run, dynamic gains may also result from the formation of a free trade area. These include increased economies of scale derived from the creation of a larger

---

[22]See Richard E. Caves and Ronald W. Jones, World Trade and Payments, chapter 15, for a complete discussion of the static trade effects resulting from a free trade area or customs union.

market, and direct foreign investment.

The existing studies examining the impact of the free
trade area between the U.S. and Israel are all empirical
exercises calculating the shifts in trade resulting from
the FTA. Due to a lack of information on domestic
prices they do not assess the domestic welfare effects
of these trade shifts.

Empirical Estimates

The most commonly used method of measuring the total net
trade expansion resulting from a free trade area is the
elasticity approach. The elasticity approach is a
partial equilibrium analysis which cannot measure the
change in the composition of bilateral trade, or the
addition of newly traded products which may result from
the FTA. In the economic literature on preferential
trading arrangements, partial equilibrium models have
typically been used to analytically evaluate, ex ante,
the direct trade effects of such arrangements.[23]   This

---

[23]For example, see Sellekaerts, W. "How meaningful
are Empirical Studies on Trade Creation and Diversion?" Weltwirtschaftliches Archiv vol. 109, 1973,
pp. 519-553. A number of articles were written on the
EEC-Israel Preferential Agreement using a partial
equilibrium model including Yaacov Cohen, "Israel
and the EEC, 1958-1978: Economic and Political Relations," in The Economic Integration of Israel in the
EEC, ed. Herbert Giersch, (Tubingen: J.C.B. Mohr (Paul
Siebeck), 1980), and Richard Pomfret and Benjamin Toren,
Israel and the European Common Market: An Appraisal of

approach requires the use of both import demand and
export supply elasticities to determine the respon-
siveness of both buyers and sellers to changes in import
duties. It is also necessary to make assumptions about
the potential price response by each country to a change
in their respective import duties. It is important to
note that there are serious data limitations in
estimating U.S. and Israeli elasticities. Without
disaggregated import price data, it is difficult to
accurately estimate the U.S. import demand elasticity
with respect to imports from Israel. Data on Israeli
import elasticities, as well as reliable estimates of
both U.S. and Israeli export supply elasticities, are
also not available.

Despite these data limitations, several authors have
conducted useful empirical exercises estimating the
trade impact of Israel entering into a free trade area
with a larger country. The first such empirical
exercise was conducted by Pomfret in his analysis of
Israel's free trade area with the EEC.[24] In analyzing
the impact on Israel's imports, Pomfret assumes infinitely elastic EEC export supply, since Israel accounts

---

the 1975 Free Trade Agreement (Tubingen: J.C.B. Mohr
(Paul Siebeck), 1980).

[24]Pomfret and Toren, Israel and the European Common
Market, Part 2.

A FREE TRADE AREA BETWEEN ISRAEL AND A LARGER COUNTRY

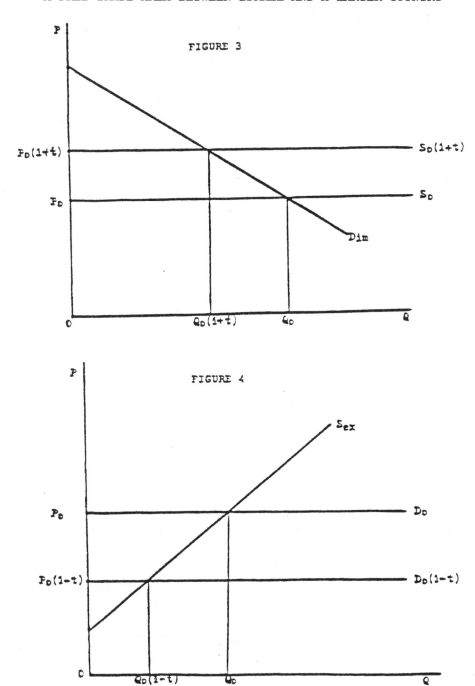

FIGURE 3

FIGURE 4

for a very small proportion of total EEC exports. He
estimates domestic demand and supply elasticities for
Israel, yielding a downward sloping import demand
curve. This approach is illustrated in Figure 3.
Pomfret concludes that Israel's domestic price on traded
goods will fall by the amount of the tariff (from
$P_{O(1+t)}$ to P_O) when tariffs on imports from the EEC are
eliminated. This implies the full pass-through of the
duty reduction to the Israeli importer.

Looking at the market for Israel's exports, Pomfret
takes a different approach. He estimates Israel's
export supply curve, yielding significantly positive
price elasticities,[25] and assumes an infinitely elastic
EEC demand for Israel's imports. This approach is
illustrated in Figure 4. An upwardly sloping supply
curve implies that Israeli exporters would be able to
increase their prices from $P_{O(1-t)}$ to P_O after the
tariff is lifted. Thus, they do not pass through any of
the tariff reduction and would increase their exports.

Pelzman's[26] article estimating the short-run trade and
employment effects of the U.S.-Israel FTA, uses U.S. im-

---

[25]Ibid.

[26]Pelzman, "The Impact of the U.S.-Israel Free
Trade Area Agreement on Israeli Trade and Employment,"
pp. 36-37.

port demand elasticities from Stern, Deardorff, and
Shiells, and uses the same elasticities to approximate
Israeli import demand elasticities.[27] He assumes that
the supply of both Israeli and U.S. exports are perfectly elastic.[28] Thus, Figure 3 represents Pelzman's
analysis of the impact of a free trade area on both
Israel's imports and exports. Since both countries are
assumed to have infinitely elastic export supply curves,
Pelzman's model implies that exporters in both the
U.S. and Israel would pass through the full extent of
any tariff reduction to the importer.

Both studies avoid dealing with two important issues for
purposes of simplification. First, because of the
difficulty in estimating cross elasticity of demand with
respect to source of imports, neither Pomfret and
Pelzman deal with the effect of third country suppliers
in their analyses. Both assume that an increase in
imports displaces domestic production but does not

---

[27]R. Stern, A. Deardorff, and C. Shiells, "Esti-
mates of the Elasticities of Substitution Between
Imports and Home Goods for the United States," Office of
Foreign Economic Research, U.S. Department of Labor,
Washington D.C., 1982.

[28]For a mathematical derivation of the model in
Figure 3, see Robert E. Baldwin and Wayne E. Lewis,
"U.S. Tariff Effects on Trade and Employment in Detailed
SIC Industries," in ed., W.G. Dewald, Impact of
International Trade and Investment on Employment,
U.S. Department of Labor, Washington D.C., 1978.

affect imports from other countries. Second, neither calculates the potential trade diversion resulting from the free trade area. Pomfret writes that economists have argued that the trade diversion effects from a free trade area are empirically unimportant in comparison with the trade creation effects.[29] Pomfret goes on to state that in the case of a small country like Israel forming an FTA with a large trading bloc like the EEC, the incidence of trade diversion harmful to Israel will be insignificant, and the specialization of production resulting from the formation of such an FTA will be welfare increasing for Israel.[30]

An important point to mention in discussing trade diversion is that upon entering into the FTA with the United States, Israel will be in the unusual position of potentially reducing any trade diversion that would have resulted from its free trade agreement with the EEC. Since Israel will be phasing in duty elimination to

---

[29]See Bela Balassa,"Trade Creation and Diversion in the European Common Market. An Appraisal of the Evidence." in ed. Bela Balassa, European Economic Integration, (Amsterdam: North Holland Publishing Co., 1975), pp.79-118.

[30]Pomfret and Toren, Israel and the European Common Market, p. 37. Since Pomfret's results indicate that Israel's FTA with the EEC will yield it significant trade creation without any significant trade diversion, he concludes that Israel will reap the majority of the gains from the Israel-EEC FTA.

U.S. imports at the same time that it will be completing
its duty elimination to imports from the EEC, the FTA
with the U.S. will minimize any substantial diversion to
imports from the EEC that might have taken place.

Comparing the approaches used by Pomfret and Pelzman, we
realize that both make the same assumptions in estimating the effect of the free trade area on Israel's
imports. The two models differ when looking at the
effect of the free trade area on Israel's exports.
Inherent in Pomfret's approach of an upward sloping
supply curve for Israel's exports, combined with a
perfectly elastic EEC demand for those exports, is the
implication that the EEC will be willing to import any
amount that Israel is willing to supply at the world
price. Given the small size of Israel's economy
relative to that of the U.S. or the EEC, its exports
will most likely be limited by its ability to supply.
Since Pelzman makes the assumption that Israel's export
supply is infinitely elastic, his analysis yields
upper-bound estimates, overstating the impact of a
tariff elimination on Israel's supply of exports.

Estimating the Trade and Employment Impact of the FTA
In examining the _ex ante_ trade effects of the FTA, it is
important to realize that since nearly 90% of Israeli

imports already entered the U.S. duty-free (under GSP and MFN), before the FTA, significant trade expansion was only possible as a result of bilateral tariff elimination in the remaining dutiable categories. The total trade expansion resulting from the agreement equals the sum of the trade expansion in each non-zero tariff category.

There has been very little empirical work on the costs and benefits expected to accrue to the U.S. and Israel as a result of the U.S.-Israel FTA. No rigorous economic analysis of the costs and benefits of the U.S.-Israel FTA was done by the U.S. government, either before making the decision to negotiate the agreement or since its implementation.[31] Only two articles have been written examining the economic impact of the FTA, one by Pelzman and one by Sawyer and Sprinkle.[32]

---

[31]The report done by the U.S. International Trade Commission was not a comprehensive economic analysis. It examined the potential impact of the FTA in certain product categories deemed import sensitive in the U.S. For a more complete discussion of the ITC report, see chapter IV, Section D. The Department of Labor calculated rough estimates of the employment effects of the FTA, but it did not do a comprehensive analysis of all the costs and benefits.

[32]W. Charles Sawyer and Richard Sprinkle, "The Trade Expansion Effects of the U.S.-Israel Free Trade Area Agreement," forthcoming in the Journal of World Trade Law.

Pelzman estimates what the level of Israeli exports would have been in 1982, if U.S. tariffs on Israeli exports had been eliminated at that time. He uses 1982 Israeli import data, and 1982 and 1983 U.S. import data, for the trade flows needed to calculate the gross trade expansion[33] effects of the FTA.[34] His results indicate an increase of $15.7 million in Israeli exports to the U.S., a little over 1% of total Israeli exports to the U.S. in 1982.[35] Since over 35% of U.S. exports to Israel were dutiable prior to the FTA, there is a larger potential economic impact resulting from elimination of Israel's tariffs to the United States. Pelzman's results indicate an increase of $130 million in U.S. exports to Israel, or 8.4% of total U.S. exports to Israel in 1982.

Concerning impact on employment, Pelzman concludes that due to the trivial increase in Israel's exports to the U.S., the employment effects would be negligible. With regard to Israel, he calculates that if Israeli tariffs

---

[33]Gross trade creation measures the total increase in trade, but does not differentiate between trade arising from trade creation or trade diversion.

[34]Pelzman does not attempt to estimate trade diversion. As such, his estimates do not reflect trade creation, but rather the gross trade expansion resulting from the FTA.

[35]Pelzman, "The Impact of the U.S.-Israel FTA," p. 41-42.

on U.S. exports were completely eliminated in 1982, it
would result in displacement of approximately 1 percent
of Israel's 1982 manufacturing sector employment.[36]

Sawyer and Sprinkle also examine the trade expansion
effects resulting from the FTA. They project that
U.S. exports to Israel will increase by $178.2 million
on a one-year static basis, and that total U.S. imports
from Israel will increase by $10.9 million. Although
like Pelzman, they assume perfectly elastic supply
curves for both the U.S. and Israel, Sawyer and Sprinkle
make different assumptions regarding demand elasticities, which accounts for the difference between the
two sets of results.[37]

Given the difficulty in estimating elasticities, the
empirical results obtained by both Pelzman, and Sawyer
and Sprinkle should be viewed as indicative rather than
definitive. Nonetheless, since their estimates of
increased imports for both the U.S. and Israel resulting
from the FTA are quite similar, they can be accepted as
approximate indicators of the trade impact of the FTA.

---

[36]Ibid., p. 44.

[37]Pelzman uses the U.S. import elasticities derived
by Stern, Deardorff, and Shiells in "Estimates of the
Elasticities of Substitution." Sawyer and Sprinkle do
not cite what demand elasticities they used in their
calculations, or how they were derived.

The U.S. Department of Labor calculated preliminary estimates of the employment impact in the U.S. as a result of the U.S.-Israel FTA.[38] They estimate that the U.S. could achieve a net gain of roughly 848 "employment opportunities" as a result of the FTA. This would result from a loss of 236 "employment opportunities" due to an increase in imports from Israel, and a gain of 1,048 "employment opportunities" as a result of increased U.S. exports to Israel. These estimates are to be taken as only approximate indications of possible U.S. employment because they estimate "job opportunities" as opposed to actual jobs, they assume constant labor-to-output coefficients, and they use general rather than productspecific elasticities.

Despite problems with some of the assumptions used and the data limitations, the three studies discussed above all point to a very small increase in Israel's exports to the United States as a result of the FTA, and a larger, but still relatively small increase in U.S. exports to Israel. Similarly, the employment impact for the U.S., as indicated by Pelzman and the Department of Labor is expected to be very small; the employment

---

[38]U.S. Department of Labor, "Employment Impact of the U.S.-Israel Free Trade Area: Preliminary Estimates," unpublished paper, Washington D.C., November 15, 1984.

impact for Israel is expected to be larger, but would only result in a displacement of 1% of the manufacturing sector. In addition, the two employment impact studies overestimate the extent of labor displacement resulting from the FTA because both assume immediate tariff elimination, while in actuality tariffs will be gradually reduced over a ten-year period. Pelzman's employment estimates also do not take into account employment created from increased exports.

Because of the difficulty in estimating Israel's supply and demand elasticities, this paper will not attempt to estimate the welfare impact of the FTA. It is safe to assume that both the consumer gains, and the producer gains and losses resulting from the FTA, will probably be more substantial for Israel than for the U.S. Since Israel had a higher level of tariffs and exports subsidies prior to the negotiation of the FTA, it will have more to gain from their elimination. For the U.S. the net social welfare gain will be relatively smaller since its domestic tariffs were already quite low. The total duties paid on Israel's exports to the United States in 1983 were only $10.2 million.[39] The total duties paid on U.S. exports to Israel were $73.7

---

[39]Pelzman, "The Impact of the U.S.-Israel FTA," p. 19.

million in 1983. To the United States, this translates
into a negligible loss in government revenue. For
Israel the loss in government revenue is somewhat
larger, but it is still not a significant amount.[40]

Evaluating the FTA's Benefits and Limitations for
the United States and Israel

Having seen the FTA's negligible trade impact on both
countries, one wonders what each country stood to gain
by negotiating the agreement. Each country had specific
reasons for entered into the FTA agreement. The primary
export benefit that Israel sought to obtain in negotiating the FTA was to preserve, on a permanent basis,
the duty-free access that 37.9% of its imports were
enjoying under the GSP program. Israel's first concern
was the uncertain future of the GSP program. Second,
the competitive-need limit of the GSP program, which
automatically cuts off GSP benefits when imports of a
given product reach a certain fraction of total imports
of that product, makes Israel dependent on the actions
of other countries. For instance, when Iran stopped

---

[40]According to the Central Bureau of Statistics,
Statistical Abstract of Israel 1984, No. 35 (Jerusalem:
Government of Israel Publications, 1984), total tax
revenue to the Israeli government in 1983 was in excess
of $11 billion dollars, and revenue from taxes on
imports was $2.4 billion, making the revenue from
tariffs on U.S. imports to Israel 3% of total government
revenue from imports, and 0.66% of total government
revenue from all sources.

exporting licorice to the U.S. after the overthrow of the Shah, Israel's share of the U.S. licorice market grew to over 50%. As a consequence, Israel lost GSP benefits for this product because its share of total U.S. imports increased, even though its exports of licorice to the U.S. did not increase absolutely. Third, while approximately 3100 U.S. tariff items are eligible for GSP treatment, a large number of products are not eligible. The following products have been specifically excluded from GSP eligibility : 1) textiles; 2) watches; 3) footwear; 4) hand bags and leather apparel; 5) import-sensitive electronic products; 6) importsensitive steel products; 7) import-sensitive glass products; and 8) any other products which the President determines to be import sensitive in his annual review of the GSP program. Finally, as a country that is rapidly becoming industrialized, Israel could be eventually "graduated" from the program altogether.[41]

Israel also hoped to gain several longer-term benefits

---

[41]The 1984 legislation mandates the President to graduate any country with a per capita GNP of $8,500 or more. With a per capita GNP of $5,890, Israel was not in immediate danger of graduation, however it would continue to be subject to the limits imposed by the competitive needs rules, as well as the "discretionary" graduation schemes. The complete rules of GSP eligibility are described in Appendix I of this chapter.

from the FTA. The first was to shift its exports away from the EEC, and towards the United States. With the accession of Spain and Portugal to the EEC, Israel will face stiff competition in many products, like citrus and olives, that it has traditionally exported to the EEC. Second, Israel hoped that the FTA would stimulate foreign investment because of its status as the only country that enjoys duty-free access to both the EEC and United States. Israeli government officials felt that the permanence of the FTA would give Israeli factories the confidence to make decisions based on continued duty-free access to the U.S. market. On the import side, Israel stands to gain by opening its market to cheaper U.S. imports.

For the United States, trade policy, rather than economics was the primary motivation for negotiating the FTA. U.S. policymakers hoped that bilateral trade liberalization would stimulate multilateral trade liberalization.[42] The key economic motivation was that the FTA would stop the perceived erosion of Israeli market share held by the United States. U.S. policy-makers felt that the EEC would gradually capture a greater proportion of the Israeli market as a result of

---

[42]For a detailed discussion of the U.S. trade policy motivations involved in the U.S. decision to negotiate the FTA, see chapter IV.

its FTA with Israel. Israel is phasing in duty reductions on EEC exports that would have made EEC products
cheaper than their American competitors in Israel.
Although Table 1 did not reveal any loss of U.S. market
share since 1980, when Israel began phasing in its
tariff elimination to the EEC, Israel's full tariff elimination to the EEC will not be completed until 1989,
and the U.S. was concerned about losses in market share
at that time. U.S. policymakers were also interested in
obtaining the elimination of some of Israel's nontariff
barriers, in particular the elimination of export
subsidies and the limitation of performance
requirements.

We noted earlier in the chapter that the amount and
impact of U.S. imports from Israel, even after the FTA,
will be very small. Looking at individual sectors
reveals that even in some of the sectors considered
"sensitive" by U.S. policymakers,[43] Israel is a very
small exporter. For example, Israel's share of U.S.
imports of textiles and apparel was 0.2% in 1981.
Moreover, in 1982, the U.S. had a $15.8 million surplus
with Israel in textile and apparel trade. In 1983,

---

[43]See chapters IV and V for a complete discussion
of what sectors were considered sensitive by U.S.
policymakers and how those sectors were treated in
the course of the FTA negotiations.

Israel's bromine exports to the U.S. accounted for 5% of all U.S. consumption of bromine and brominated products. In 1983, the U.S. exported $306 million worth of agricultural products to Israel while imports from Israel amounted to only $55 million, 0.3% of the total U.S. agricultural imports that year.[44] In addition, the distance, and consequent high costs of transportation and risk of spoilage are a constraint on Israeli agricultural exports to the United States. Even with tariff elimination, closer markets like Europe will continue to be the major outlet for Israel's food-stuffs. It is doubtful that the United States will experience any significant structural adjustment in any product sectors as a result of the FTA.

The modest potential for trade expansion by both Israel and the United States is even more apparent in view of the extensive nontariff barriers that were not eli-minated by the FTA. Because the agreement allows each side to maintain its quotas, Israel will still be faced with U.S. agricultural quotas, and the comprehensive textile quotas under the Multifiber Arrangement. Since textiles and agriculture are the two key sectors where Israel did not already enjoy duty-free access to the

---

[44]Office of the U.S. Trade Representative statistics.

United States before the FTA, these are the two sectors where it had the most potential for trade expansion.

Pelzman projects changes in Israel's exports to the United States that would have occurred in 1982, if U.S. tariffs on Israeli exports had been eliminated at that time. Table 5 is a list, derived from that calculation, of the Israeli products that were projected to have increased exports of $100,000 or more when U.S. tariffs were eliminated. Of the twenty-three items with the highest predicted increase in exports, thirteen are textile items and five are agricultural products. In addition to the nontariff barriers still facing textile items, the majority are in the third tranche of tariff elimination in the FTA, which means that they will not be duty free until 1995. Of the remaining products on the list, tomato sauce, preserved or prepared tomatoes, two categories of gold jewelry, and olives are all in the fourth tranche, with tariffs frozen until 1995. Cheese, which is in the second tranche, is also under quota. Thus almost all the items with potential for significant trade expansion are in the later stages of tariff elimination and most are under quota.

TABLE 5

**PROJECTED CHANGES IN ISRAEL'S 1982 DUTIABLE EXPORTS TO
THE U.S. RESULTING FROM A COMPLETE ELIMINATION OF
U.S. TARIFFS**

TSUSA (ranked by total value)	Description	Increase in Israel's exports (thousands of dollars)	U.S. tariff rate (percent)
38384	women's swim suits over $10	2,985	30.3
38386	knit man-made fiber apparel	1,194	32.9
14165	tomato sauce	1,028	13.6
38306	women's cotton suits	927	32.7
38383	women's swim suits under $10	802	32.8
68610	parts of resistors	752	6.0
14166	tomatoes, prepared or preserved	461	14.7
74013	necklaces and chains	375	9.9
74014	jewelry of precious metals	333	9.9
61049	iron or steel pipes and tubes	327	10.1
38320	women's knit apparel	202	39.7
38380	women's and girl's sweaters	195	34.7
79176	other wearing apparel	179	6.0
37460	man-made fiber hosiery	175	36.2
11788	cheese and substitutes	143	10.0
31091	sewing thread and yarn	141	20.5
37976	men's and boy's wool apparel	137	21.2
70053	footwear	131	37.5
38381	women's and girl's knit shorts	122	32.5
38330	women's cotton apparel	111	18.8
37815	women's knit underwear	105	13.7
16730	grape wine	103	6.6
14850	olives	101	7.0

Source: Office of the U.S. Trade Representative trade
statistics, excerpted from Pelzman (1985).

nontariff barrier to Israeli exports not addressed by
the FTA. U.S. companies are free to pursue anti-dumping
(AD) and countervailing duty (CVD) cases against Israeli
products that enter the United States. Furthermore,
with the provisions in the Trade and Tariff Act of 1984,
these regulations have become increasingly stringent.
One new provision, known as "cummulation," specifies
that any country can be subject to AD or CVD proceedings, even if it is a very minor exporter of the
product covered by the case.[45] Since the FTA has been
in force, AD and CVD cases have been filed against cut
flowers, oil-country tubular goods, and industrial acid
from Israel.[46] The existence of these laws effectively
diminishes any potential gains from the FTA, because the
tariff benefits may, at any time, be negated by the
application of AD or CVD duties. The FTA also does not
limit the right of the U.S. to implement an escape
clause case on a product and limit imports of that
product from all countries, including Israel.

---

[45]For instance, although Israel's exports of cut
roses only amounted to 1.6% of total U.S. imports, they
were included in the countervailing duty case filed
against Colombia, the largest exporter of cut roses to
the U.S. As a result, Israel now faces a 22.6% duty on
its exports of cut roses, a much more significant
barrier to trade than the original 8% tariff.

[46]Cases filed with the U.S. International Trade
Commission.

Israel also has some very substantial nontariff barriers
that are not covered by the FTA. Israel's most important nontariff barrier, the TAMA, is often a more
onerous tax on imports than the tariff. Pelzman
calculated the impact of the TAMA on U.S. exports to
Israel.[47] His calculations showed that while an
elimination of Israel's tariffs, at the 1982 level of
trade, would have resulted in an increase in U.S. exports of $130 million, or 8.4%, if one adds elimination
of the TAMA to the equation, the increase in U.S. exports jumps to $284.8 million, or an increase of 18.4%.
On total 1982 U.S. exports to Israel of $1,546 million,
the duties charged were $73.7 million, however, the
"hidden tariff" imposed on U.S. imports represented an
additional levy of $130.6 million. In addition, the
existence of the TAMA provides the Israeli government
with total discretion to continue to protect items whose
tariffs are being eliminated. According to Israeli
customs officials, both the TAMA rates and the purchasing taxes have been raised to compensate for some of
the tariff reductions necessitated by the Israel-EEC
FTA.[48] Based on this experience, one could expect the
Israeli government to raise the TAMA rates in a number

_____

[47]Pelzman, "The Impact of the U.S.-Israel Free
Trade Area," pp. 26-30, 42-46.

[48]Ibid., p. 29.

of key sectors in order to compensate for some of the
tariff elimination imposed by the U.S.-Israel FTA.
While it is unclear to what extent the TAMA rates would
be raised, such actions would clearly have the potential
to negate the impact of some or all of Israel's tariff
reductions resulting from the FTA.

D. Conclusions

While the FTA has elements that provide some economic
benefits to both sides-- notably, permanent duty-free
access for GSP products for Israel, and tariff preferences for the United States equivalent to the EEC's--
the projected impact resulting from the elimination of
tariffs will be small for the U.S., and even smaller for
Israel. Furthermore, these potential gains resulting
from bilateral tariff elimination are substantially
diminished by extensive nontariff barriers on both
sides. Yet, despite the modest economic impact of the
FTA, its negotiation was frought with obstacles and
political resistance, as we shall see in the following
chapters.

APPENDIX I

The U.S. Generalized System of Preferences: Rules of Eligibility

In the GSP program, as was enacted in Title V of the Trade Act of 1974, a GSP recipient's exports to the U.S. of a given product would cease to receive preferential treatment if, in a calendar year: a) they exceeded in value an absolute dollar limit or b) they accounted for 50% or more of the value of U.S. imports of that product. The statute set the limit at $25 million for 1974. After that, the limit was to increase each year by indexing the original limit by the ratio of the preceding GNP to that of the 1974 GNP and multiplying by $25 million. Thus, the dollar value of the "competitive need" limit was:

Year	Limit (millions of $)
1975	26.6
1976	29.9
1977	33.4
1978	37.3
1979	41.9
1980	45.8
1981	50.9
1982	53.0
1983	57.0

Section 1111 of the Trade Agreements Act of 1979 amended the statute to waive the 50% limit for products in which U.S. imports were valued at less than $1 million in 1979. This level is also adjusted annually to reflect growth in GNP. In 1982, the level was $1.26 million.

The Trade and Tariff Act of 1984, specified that most of the present limits would hold until January 4, 1987, at which time, the President was authorized to review all eligible products under the program, and is to lower by 50% the competitive needs limits on a product-specific basis, if he determined that the recipient has demonstrated "a sufficient degree of competitiveness with respect to any eligible article." Furthermore, the new legislation added a country graduation clause, whereby the President is required to graduate any country with a per capita GNP of $8,500 or more (indexed annually to 50% of the change in the U.S. GNP), phasing them out over a two year period.

The requirements for GSP eligibility were tightened in 1981 when it introduced a scheme which specified discretionary criteria for "graduating" a product from GSP eligibility. Under this scheme, the President can consider whether the level of economic development of the recipient is above some unspecified level, or whether it is competitive in the product concerned, and/or whether the overall economic interests of the United States, including the import sensitivity of the domestic industry, require the product's removal from GSP.

APPENDIX II

The Provisions of the U.S.-Israel FTA

All commercial trade between the United States and Israel will be covered by the Agreement, and all duties will be phased out over ten years. This will be accomplished in four phases:

1) Elimination of duties on some products immediately upon the agreement's entry into force.

2) Elimination of duties on some products in three stages by January 1, 1989. There will be an initial duty reduction (see below) when the agreement enters into force, from which there will be a 60% percent reduction on January 1, 1987 and a 40% reduction (to zero duty) on January 1, 1989. Initial duty reductions on U.S. imports from Israel will fall into two categories: if the product was part of the Tokyo Round of Trade Negotiations, the final MTN rate will be provided to Israeli products immediately; if the product was not, an initial cut of 20% will be made when the agreement enters into force, establishing a new base for the future reductions. Israeli imports from the United States will receive the preferential rate provided to the European Community under the Israel-EEC Preferential

Agreement. The Israel-EEC agreement legally prohibits Israel from providing treatment to any other countries which is better than the treatment provided to the EEC during the phase in of that agreement.

3) Elimination of duties on some products in eight stages by January 1, 1995. There will be a 20% tariff cut upon the agreement's entry into force, a 10% cut on 1/1/86, a 10% cut on 1/1/87, a 10% cut on 1/1/88, a 10% cut on 1/1/89, a 10% cut on 1/1/90, a 20% cut on 1/1/92, and complete duty elimination on 1/1/95.

4) Freezing of duties on some products for five years. Products in this category were deemed by both sides as sensitive in the context of the agreement. After five years, the President will seek the advice of the ITC as to the timetable of tariff elimination on the U.S. products. Both the United States and Israel have agreed to bring these products under the agreement by January 1, 1995.

Summary of the key nontariff sections of the agreement:
Article 4: Restricts the rights of either nation to impose new restrictions on the other's trade, unless specifically permitted by the FTA or the GATT.
Article 5: Addresses the application of the safeguard

provision of GATT Article XIX and brings the FTA into conformity with the safeguards provision of the Trade and Tariff Act of 1984.

Article 6: Provides that both countries may maintain import restrictions if based on agricultural policy considerations.

Article 8: Provides for a special exception for trade measures maintained by either nation relating to religious prohibitions, i.e., Kosher restrictions.

Article 10: Allows Israel to apply protective measures to protect infant industries until 1995. Israel may increase or introduce duties up to 20% on a maximum of 10% of 1984 U.S. exports to Israel through 12/31/1990. Such tariffs must be reduced at least 5% annually 24 months after imposition and eliminated by 1/1/1995. This restricts some of the rights Israel has under Article XVIII of the GATT.

Article 11: Authorizes the application by either party of temporary restrictions in serious balance of payments (BOP) situations, but limits such measures in the form of quantitative restrictions to 300 days, and in the form of import surcharges to 150 days unless extended by legislation for additional 150 day periods. These limitations are more restrictive than the GATT BOP provisions under Articles XII and XVIII.

Article 12: Prohibits the imposition of import licensing requirements unless they are automatically approved or are necessary to administer quantitative or other restrictions consistent with the FTA or the GATT. Parties are required to exchange lists of items subject to license, and provide justification for any license denial within 60 days. These procedures are more restrictive than those contained in the GATT Code on Import Licensing Procedures.

Article 13: Prohibits the imposition of export or domestic purchase performance requirements on investment.

Article 15: Both countries are signatories to the GATT Government Procurement Code which requires to waive their buy-national restrictions on a broad range of government purchases. Under the FTA, both agree to further lower, on a bilateral basis the threshold for application of the code from 150,000 SDRs (about $156,000) to $50,000. Israel will also include non-military purchases by its Ministry of Defense, which are currently not covered by the GATT Agreement on Government Procurement, and liberalize its offset requirements, on all civilian agency purchases.

Article 16: States that both countries recognize the importance of trade in services and agree to develop a means of cooperation pursuant to a separate Declaration on Services.

Article 20: Provides that each nation may increase the value of its specific duties when the value of their currency decreases more than 20%, in order to maintain the same duty levels set out in the FTA.

IV.   The Trade Policy Process

This chapter examines the motivations and policy process in the United States that led to the negotiation and implementation of the U.S.-Israel Free Trade Area.   In order to understand the trade policy process involved in the negotiation and implementation of the FTA, the first section of this chapter digresses briefly to examine the interaction between the Executive branch and the Congress in the trade policy process, and in particular with regard to trade agreements.   In the United States, the policy process of achieving a free trade area with Israel started in the Executive branch with the decision in November 1983 by President Reagan and Prime Minister Shamir to negotiate a free trade area.

The second section of the chapter examines the history of U.S. trade policy and the events that played a role in pushing both countries toward the decision to negotiate a free trade area.   Once this decision was made, negotiations commenced and the U.S. trade policy process shifted to the decision of how the agreement would be implemented into U.S. law.   The role of Congress in the negotiation of the FTA is discussed in the third section of the chapter.   Two important

remaining elements of the trade policy process are the
International Trade Commission (ITC) and the role of
pressure groups. The fourth section of this chapter
analyzes the role of the ITC, and in particular the
impact its report on the FTA had on the domestic trade
policy process and on the negotiations. The chapter
concludes with a discussion of the role that pressure
groups played in informing and influencing all the
branches of government, and as a result, in the negotiation and implementation of the FTA.

A.   The Partnership Between Congress and the Executive in the Trade Policy Process

Under the United States Constitution, commercial relations are the province of the Congress although it is
the President who negotiates with foreign countries.
Any trade agreement that the President negotiates must
be implemented into U.S. law by the Congress. Trade
negotiations are thus conducted in the context of a
delicate political partnership between the President and
Congress. The requirement for Congress to pass legislation implementing any agreement the President negotiates has led to a fifty-year precedent of Congress
granting the President explicit statutory authority to

negotiate.[1]

The President is not constitutionally prohibited from negotiating an international trade accord and then presenting it as an executive agreement to the Congress for implementing legislation.[2] Historically, however, for political rather than constitutional reasons, the President and the Congress have accepted that trade agreements should generally be negotiated based on the prior authority of both houses of Congress, and then presented to the Congress for implementing legislation. Such Congressional-Eexecutive branch agreements have the advantage of eliminating the danger that the President would negotiate an agreement that the Congress would not be willing to implement into United States law.

The Congress may also choose to delegate authority to the President to proclaim tariff changes, in which case

---

[1]Historically, Congress set tariff levels on an item-by- item basis. In the Trade Agreements Act of 1934, Congress authorized the President to negotiate trade agreements with other countries and granted him the power to reduce duties by as much as 50%. This action was significant because it marked an end to detailed tariff setting by Congress on a comprehensive basis. For a discussion of the historical relationship between Congress and the President on tariff policy, see Robert E. Baldwin, The Political Economy of U.S. Import Policy, (Cambridge: Massachusettes Institute of Technology Press, 1985), chapter 2.

[2]United States Constitution, Article VI, section 2.

the President does not need to bring the changes back to
1Congress to implement into law; rather he can implement
them into U.S. law through proclamation. When the
Congress has delegated proclamation authority in the
past, it has generally placed limitations on that
authority so as to maintain some control over the negotiations process.[3] This need for implementing legislation or proclamation authority has created an important role for Congress in trade negotiations.
Congressional involvement is also important because
foreign governments are aware of the need for Congressional support and are unlikely to be willing to
enter into serious trade negotiations with the President
if they do not believe he has Congressional support.

Since the Trade Agreements Act of 1934, Congress has
periodically extended the authority of the President to
reduce tariffs on a reciprocal basis and has provided
him with additional tariffcutting authority. This
authority, however, has generally been granted for only
short periods of time and has been circumscribed in

---

[3]For example, in the Trade Act of 1974 which gave
the President authority to negotiate in the Tokyo Round,
section 101 specified that the President may not agree
to reduce duties to "a rate below 40% of the rate
existing on January 1, 1975." Furthermore, since the
nontariff barrier negotiating authority required the
President to bring that portion of the agreement
back to Congress for implementation, Congress had
leverage to monitor the entire package of negotiations.

various ways, providing Congress the opportunity to
periodically stop further duty reductions. In granting
such authority, Congress has tried to avoid the political risks of detailed trade policymaking, yet ensure
that Congressional intentions are closely followed.
Congress has also used the renewal of authority as an
occasion to restrict the tariff-cutting authority of the
President in various ways.[4]

In the Trade Act of 1974, Congress gave the President
tariffcutting authority (section 101), a provision which
served as the basis for negotiation of tariff reductions
in the Tokyo Round.[5] This provision allowed the
President to proclaim tariff reductions within certain
set parameters. This act also directed the President to
seek revisions of the GATT with regard to twelve
specific nontariff barriers.[6]

Most significantly, the Trade Act of 1974 required the
President to consult with the members of the House Ways
and Means Committee and Senate Finance Committee, as
well as other relevant Congressional committees, prior

---

[4]Baldwin, The Political Economy of U.S. Import
Policy, p. 35.

[5]The Trade Act of 1974, section 101(a)(1).

[6]The Trade Act of 1974, section 102.

to concluding nontariff trade agreements, and to submit
these agreements for approval to both houses of Congress. It is important to note that while the President
could simply proclaim the tariff changes negotiated in
the Tokyo Round, he had to send the nontariff portion of
the package to Congress for approval. This effectively
meant that Congress could also exert control over the
tariff negotiations by holding the nontariff portion of
the package hostage.[7]

In requiring the President to submit the nontariff
agreements to Congress for approval, Congress had to
deal with its proclivity to amend implementing legislation. This creates particular problems when an
agreement has been carefully negotiated and concessions
delicately balanced. In recognition of this problem,
the Congress enacted section 151 of the Trade Act of
1974.[8] This provision established "fast track" procedures for consideration of legislation to implement the
Tokyo Round agreements. These procedures forbade
amendments to legislation, forcing Congress to simply
vote between complete approval or rejection of the
implementing legislation. The advantage of this

---

[7]For a detailed discussion of the Congressional
approval of the Trade Act of 1974, see Baldwin, The
Political Economy of U.S. Import Policy, pp.53-77.

[8]The Trade Act of 1974, section 151.

provision is that it allows swift enactment of trade agreements, avoiding the years of deliberation generally accompanying complex legislation, and also assures the President and foreign governments that the agreement will be considered in the form agreed upon by the parties.

Because the legislation must be approved or rejected in its entirety, neither Congress nor the President wants an agreement submitted until they are reasonably certain that it will be approved. This creates a situation where the President must work closely with Congress throughout the negotiation process in order to ensure that he negotiates an agreement that Congress will be willing to implement into law.

This process of informal consultation reduces the transparency in the policy process since many of the issues are resolved informally between both branches, rather than being explicitly stated in amendments or detailed authority. This close working relationship operates on two levels, with Cabinet members and political appointees consulting with the Congressmen during a negotiation process, and civil servants in the agencies consulting with Congressional staff.

The members of Congress likely to have the greatest influence over trade issues are those who serve on the committees with the relevant legislative authority, principally the House Ways and Means Committee and the Senate Finance Committee.[9] Although this has always been the case because of the expertise these members develop about trade issues (especially those serving on the trade subcommittees of the broader committees), in a situation like the "fast track" procedure where the President must consult and work with these committee members before officially submitting a trade agreement, it becomes more pronounced.[10]

In the Executive branch, the lead agency for trade negotiations is the Office of the United States Trade Representative (USTR), which is in the Executive Office of the President. While USTR has the lead, trade policy decisions in the Executive branch are made through an interagency process which operates on several levels. Each agency brings to the process its own perspective as it seeks to represent its "constituency" in the decision making process. The other key agencies involved in the

---

[9]Baldwin, The Political Economy of U.S. Import Policy, p.50.

[10]For a list of the members of the Trade Subcommittees of the House Ways and Means and Senate Finance Committees during the U.S.-Israel FTA proceedings, see Appendix I to this chapter.

interagency process on trade policy issues,[11] are: the
Commerce Department, which represents the interests of
U.S. industry in the trade policy process, deals with
trade in manufactured goods, as well as with industry
requests for import protection on grounds of dumping,
subsidization, and national security; the Agriculture
Department, which represents the interests of the U.S.
agricultural community, concentrates on trade in
agricultural goods; the Labor Department, which represents the interests of the domestic labor force,
concerns itself with the impact of trade on domestic
labor; the State Department, which handles U.S. relationships with foreign countries, focuses on the impact
trade policy decisions will have on those relationships;
and the Treasury Department, which deals with the
collection of duties, exchange rates, and other international monetary matters.

Although these are the major agencies, a number of other

---

[11]There are a number of interagency groups headed
by agencies involved with trade. The Trade Policy
Committee (TPC) and its subcommittees is run by the
USTR, and is the body charged with overseeing trade
negotiations. The Cabinet Council on Commerce and Trade
(CCCT) is headed by the Secretary of Commerce. After
James Baker became the Secretary of the Treasury, a new
Cabinet level interagency group, the Economic Policy
Committee, headed by the Treasury Department became a
key interagency trade policy decision-making group.
Since the FTA negotiations were headed by the USTR it
was the TPC that was the decision-making body during the
negotiation process.

agencies also get involved in trade issues. A representative from the Justice Department sits on the Trade
Policy Subcommittee (TPSC), and has an interest in
issues such as international antitrust. A representative from the Office of Management and Budget sits
on the TPSC, and monitors policy initiatives that will
require budgetary allocations. There are also representatives from the Council of Economic Advisors, and
the National Security Council, both part of the
Executive Office of the President, and occasionally from
the Defense Department, when certain trade policy issues
are believed to have national security implications.
Other agencies, such as the Environmental Protection
Agency and the Food and Drug Administration get involved
in issues that fall within their purview.

On the Cabinet level, the Trade Policy Committee,
chaired by the USTR is comprised of the key agencies
discussed above, plus any additional agencies relevant
to the particular matter at hand. On the subcabinet
level, the Trade Policy Review Group is chaired by the
Deputy USTR. Below the Trade Policy Review Group, there
is the Trade Policy Subcommittee (TPSC), chaired by the
Assistant USTR. Finally, there is the Trade Policy
Subcommittee Working Group that is chaired by a staff
person from USTR in charge of a particular issue. It

was this hierarchy of interagency committees that made
decisions during the FTA negotiation process. The
working group makes day-to-day decisions which are
brought before the TPSC for approval. In the case of
larger policy decisions, or where the TPSC cannot agree,
the matter is brought before the Trade Policy Review
Group or the Trade Policy Committee.

The third part of the U.S. government that plays a role
in the formulation of trade policy is the U.S. International Trade Commission (ITC). The ITC was established in 1916 by the Congress to provide it and the
President with expert and impartial information in the
formulation of trade policy. The Commission is composed
of six commissioners appointed by the President and is
supported by a professional staff. As an independent,
quasi-judicial agency, the ITC makes recommendations to
the President concerning import relief in escape clause
cases, and conducts studies at the request of the
Executive or Legislative branches concerning the impact
of trade policies.

Summary
Because Congress must answer to its constituents on any
trade agreement that it eventually passes into law,
Congress uses various legislative tools, such as the

"fast track" procedure, to exert as much control as possible over trade negotiations. Congressmen, particularly those on key committees, try to ensure that trade agreements have exceptions or allowances for politically sensitive industries in their districts. Generally, an industry that has been protected in one trade agreement will continue to be protected in future trade agreements; this protection becomes politically entrenched and no Congressmen wants to take the political risk of ending that protection.

The implication for trade negotiations is that U.S. negotiators are guided by a desire to negotiate an agreement that maintains protection on politically sensitive items, thus minimizing the opposition in Congress. This generally results in liberalizing agreements with individual protectionist exceptions, designed to accommodate pressures on key groups of Congressmen.

The Executive branch usually tries to balance what it has to concede to obtain agreement from its trading partners in a negotiation, with what it can sell domestically to the Congress. It will often use the protective stance of Congress as a tool in negotiating with foreign countries. The threat that Congress will

pass protectionist legislation has often been used by
the Executive branch to extract import restraint
agreements from trading partners, and the admonition
that Congress will never approve an agreement that is
too lenient has been used to obtain concessions when
negotiating trade agreements. This ritual allows
Congress to appear tough to its constituents and allows
the administration to lay the blame on Congress for any
concessions it is unable to make. Conversely, it also
allows the Congress to blame the Administration when an
agreement is negotiated that is too liberal to suit its
constituents.

B.   The Decision To Negotiate A Free Trade Area

The history of the post-World War II international
trading system, under the auspices of the General
Agreement on Tariffs and Trade (GATT), has been based on
the most-favorednation (MFN) principle. According to
this principle, all nations that are signatories to the
GATT are "most-favorednations" and therefore must
receive the same tariff treatment.[12] A signatory
country can only give a tariff preference to another

---

[12]GATT Article 1. For a more detailed discussion
on the MFN clause, the reader is referred to John
H. Jackson, World Trade and the Law of GATT, (New
York: Bobbs-Merrill Co., 1969), chapter 11.

signatory country if it gives the same tariff treatment
to all the other signatories; GATT Article XXIV provides
for a major exception to this rule in the case of free
trade areas or customs unions, such as in the case of
the European Economic Community.[13] The United States,
however, has traditionally been a staunch supporter of
multilateral, as opposed to bilateral trade liberalization, and opposed exceptions to the MFN principle.[14]

Since World War II, gradual multilateral tariff liberalization has taken place in the context of periodic
"rounds"-- multilateral negotiations that succeeded in
gradually lowering global tariff levels.[15] The most
recent, the Tokyo Round, completed in 1979, went a step
further by drafting codes designed to reduce nontariff

---

[13]GATT Article 24, paragraph 8(a) allows for an
exception to MFN for customs unions, defined as an
association of nations with treatment for imports from
members and a common level of external tariffs for
imports from nonmembers.

[14]For a detailed account of U.S. policy with regard
to MFN exceptions such as the EEC, see Jan Tumlir,
Protectionism: Trade Policy in Democratic Societies,
(Washington D.C.: American Enterprise Institute, 1985),
chapter 2.

[15]There have been seven major rounds of GATT tariff
negotiations, including the first which was conducted
while the GATT itself was being drafted. This initial
round was concluded in 1947. A second round was
completed in 1948, a third round in 1950, and a fourth
round was concluded in 1956. The fifth, the "Dillon
Round", took place from 1960 to 1961. The "Kennedy
Round" took place from 1964 to 1967, and most recently,
the "Tokyo Round" took place from 1973 to 1979.

barriers. During 1982, the United States prepared an agenda for a new round of multilateral trade liberalization talks, which it hoped would be endorsed by other major trading partners and launched at the GATT ministerial meeting in November 1982.

The United States, however, was unsuccessful in convincing other countries to adopt a workplan towards liberalization. It became clear that a majority of the GATT member countries were not receptive to further trade liberalization. A number of developed countries, in particular many European countries hurt by the economic recession, were actually moving towards increased protection. The developing world, feeling the effect of the recession in the North in the form of shrinking markets for its exports, was equally reluctant to join in any liberalization, particularly given its feeling that it had not gotten the better end of the deal in previous rounds of liberalization.

The failure of the GATT ministerial cast into question the future of multilateral trade liberalization, and officials in the U.S. trade bureaucracy began searching for alternative methods to further trade liberalization.[16]   U.S. government officials felt very strongly

that if movement in the direction of liberalization was

not sustained, there would be movement toward increased

protection.   After the U.S. government's failure at the

GATT ministerial, the U.S. Trade Representative (USTR),

William E. Brock, picked up on the idea of bilateral

liberalization as a potential impetus for other coun-

tries to join a multilateral trade liberalization

effort, and began to advocate the idea within the

Administration.

Individuals in the Israeli government had been contem-

plating the possibility of a free trade area with the

United States for some time.   The Israeli government

proposed the idea originally when they were negotiating

their preference agreement with the EEC in the early

1970s.   This was before the inception of the GSP

program, and Israel was interested in increased access

to the U.S. market.[17]   At that time, the U.S. rejected

the idea, saying that it was not interested in any

---

[16]Doral Cooper and Nancy Adams, "Overview of the
U.S.-Israel Free Trade Area Negotiations: An American
Perspective," in a forthcoming book, eds. A. Samet and
M. Goldberg, (Washington D.C.: International Law
Institute, 1988).

[17]Moshe Semadar, former Director for North American
Affairs, Ministry of International Trade and Industry,
interview by author, Jerusalem, May 6, 1985.
Mr. Semadar was Israel's lead negotiator on the FTA.

bilateral arrangements.

The U.S. enacted the GSP program into law in Title V of the Trade Act of 1974.[18] Initially authorized for ten years, it was renewed, with tighter requirements, for eight and one-half years in the Trade and Tariff Act of 1984. Growing opposition to the program by domestic industry, labor, and an increasingly protectionist Congress plagued the program. These groups were opposed to the GSP beneficiaries whose exports were successfully competing in the U.S. market against domestic products. The effect of this opposition served to endanger the program's renewal and to tighten up its requirements.[19]

Israel proposed the concept of a free trade area again in early 1981 when it became concerned about the changes to, and the future of the GSP program. The Israeli Government realized that it had one of the highest per capita GNP among the GSP beneficiaries, and that it was reaching the legislated limits under the GSP program in several areas. Israel suggested the idea as a follow-up to the Camp David Accords, in the context of a three-way free trade area between the United States, Israel, and

---

[18]Trade Act of 1974, Title V.

[19]GSP eligibility was tightened in 1981 and again in 1984. See Appendix I to chapter III for a complete discussion of the GSP rules of eligibility.

Egypt, or as an alternative, two two-way free trade
areas between the U.S. and Israel and between the
U.S. and Egypt.[20]

The Trade Policy Committee, chaired by USTR Brock, met
to consider the FTA in late 1981. Preliminary consultations were held with the Israeli government and the
Congress in early 1981. Concerns were expressed in the
Defense Department and in the State Department that an
FTA with Israel might worsen relations with the Arab
countries. Quiet inquiries were made with both Egypt
and Saudi Arabia as to their interest in a bilateral FTA
with the U.S., and the extent of their concern about a
U.S.Israel FTA. Both countries responded that they were
not interested in an FTA with the U.S. and that they
were not overly concerned about the prospect of a
U.S.-Israel FTA.[21] Although Egypt rejected the idea for
its own economic reasons, the United States did not want
to reject Israel and began to explore the possibility of
a two-way free trade area between the two countries.
Israel continued to push the idea as it became in-

---

[20]Cooper and Adams, "Overview of the U.S.-Israel
Free Trade Area," pg. 1.

[21]Doral Cooper, Assistant U.S. Trade Representative
for Africa, Middle East, and Asia, Office of the
U.S. Trade Representative, interview by author,
Washington D.C., January 9, 1985.

creasingly concerned about losing GSP benefits.

After the preliminary international and domestic consultations, the FTA was taken up for discussion by the
Cabinet Council on Commerce and Trade (CCCT), an
interagency cabinetlevel group, chaired by Secretary of
Commerce, Malcolm Baldrige, in May 1982.[22] The CCCT
recommended that the President approve the negotiation
of the FTA, and the President gave that approval in June
1982. USTR Brock already had a trip scheduled to Israel
and Egypt to inform both governments of the U.S. decision to proceed with a U.S.-Israel FTA. In the same
month, however, Israel invaded Lebanon. It was decided
in the White House that this was not the proper time to
announce this decision, and Brock was told not to go to
Israel. He went only to Egypt and did not discuss the
FTA.[23]

Throughout 1983, White House concerns about improving
relations with Israel made the FTA look more attrac-
tive. This timing coincided with the failure of the
GATT Ministerial, and the consequent interest of the

---

[22]Norman Bailey, former Special Assistant on
International Trade, National Security Council, interview by author, Washington D.C., January 10, 1985.

[23]Geoffrey Kemp, former Director of Middle East
Affairs, National Security Council, interview by author,
Washington D.C., January 16, 1985.

trade bureaucracy in the idea of bilateral liberalization. Administration trade officials began examining
a policy of bilateral trade liberalization as a potential impetus for convincing other countries to join a
multilateral trade liberalization effort. In March
1983, Israel's Minister of Industry and Trade Gideon
Patt and USTR William E. Brock met to discuss Israel's
proposal for a two-way free trade area with the United
States.[24] Given the problems the U.S. was encountering
with regard to multilateral liberalization, the free
trade area proposal was viewed with increasing favor by
Brock who suggested a round of exploratory talks and
began to advocate the idea within the Administration. Other Administration trade officials, such as
Under Secretary of Commerce Lionel Olmer, joined the
effort and began to see a free trade area with Israel as
an avenue for advancing multilateral trade policy goals.

In August 1983, the Director of the Office for North
American Affairs in Israel's Ministry of Trade and
Industry visited the United States and held informal
meetings with USTR staff to discuss the concept of a
free trade area, and how Israel's FTA with the EEC was

---

[24]Cooper and Adams, "Overview of the U.S.-Israel
Free Trade Area," p. 2.

working.[25]   During this period, USTR Brock consulted
with the leaders of the House Ways and Means Committee
and the Senate Finance Committee in order to assess the
potential support for a free trade area with Israel.[26]
After these talks, the TPSC began analyzing the merits
of negotiating a free trade area with Israel.   On
November 22, 1983, the issue was addressed by the TPC,
chaired by USTR Brock, and a recommendation to proceed
was forwarded to President Reagan the next day.[27]

USTR Brock was interested in a policy of bilateral trade
liberalization with any interested country.   He hoped
that such a policy would provide the necessary impetus
to the multilateral trade system.   Israel was seen by
the Administration as the perfect candidate for negotiating the first FTA.   First, its economy is small, so
it was hoped that there would be minimal opposition from
the U.S. domestic industry concerned about a flood of
imports into the United States.   Second, because of its
small economy, negotiating such a comprehensive agreement would be much less complex than with a more major

---

[25]Ibid.

[26]Nancy Adams, Director for Middle East Affairs,
Office of the U.S. Trade Representative, interview by
author, Washington D.C., September 5, 1985. Adams was
the lead staff level negotiator for the United States.

[27]Cooper and Adams, "Overview of the U.S.-Israel
Free Trade Area," p. 3.

U.S. trading partner. Third, and probably most importantly, it was judged that an FTA with Israel would have
the best chance of winning the necessary Congressional
approval. The Administration also viewed the FTA as
consistent with Reagan's free trade approach to international trade.

During the same period, Congress came under increasing
pressure from constituents and labor leaders concerned
about the rapidly mounting U.S. trade deficit, the high
value of the dollar, and the widening perception that
other countries were engaging in unfair trade actions.
Many believed that the U.S. was the only country that
was implementing the liberalizations agreed to in the
Tokyo Round, in spirit as well as letter. Consequently,
the Administration was concerned that it would be almost
impossible to get Congress to agree to any U.S. trade
liberalization measures. It was judged that Congress
would be willing to grant the Administration the
necessary negotiating authority for an FTA with Israel
because of the well-known Congressional support for that
country. Congressional members could be perceived as
"doing something good for Israel," with relatively
little cost at home.

There were some concerns within the trade bureaucracy

about departing from the traditional emphasis on multi-lateralism and breaking the most-favored-nation principle. While certain individuals were concerned with the potential precedent-setting effect, the mood after the GATT Ministerial was that traditional methods of trade liberalization were no longer working. As a result, when both the USTR and the Secretary of Commerce backed the FTA, the idea met with relatively little opposition.

By mid-1983, the White House was working towards a strategy for cementing relations with Israel. In anticipation of Prime Minister Shamir's visit in late 1983, the NSC prepared a package of measures designed to forge a "new strategic relationship" between the two countries, composed of a number of defense understandings and the policy option prepared by the trade bureaucracy to begin negotiations on a free trade area.[28] On November 29, 1983, during Prime Minister Shamir's visit with President Reagan, the package of measures was announced, and with it the agreement to negotiate a free trade area between the two countries. The initial goal of both leaders was to complete the agreement by Labor Day, 1984, before the elections in both the United

---

[28]Kemp interview, January 16, 1985.

States and Israel.[29]

C. The Role of Congress in the U.S.-Israel FTA

The Delegation of Negotiation Authority

After the United States and Israel announced their agreement to negotiate a free trade area, questions in the Administration began to arise regarding how to obtain the necessary negotiating authority. In order to negotiate the FTA agreement the President needed authority to negotiate reductions in both tariff and nontariff barriers. The tariff-cutting authority in the Trade Act of 1974 expired on January 2, 1980 and had not been renewed. The nontariff barrier negotiating authority was renewed until January 3, 1988 in the Trade Agreements Act of 1979.[30]

The USTR began discussing with members of Congress the need for negotiating authority for the proposed FTA in January 1984.[31] The Administration thought that

---

[29]Adams interview, July 31, 1985.

[30]Alexander H. Platt, "Free Trade With Israel: A Legislative History," in a forthcoming book, eds. A. Samet and M. Goldberg, (Washington D.C.: International Law Institute, 1988).

[31]Ibid.

obtaining broad tariff-cutting authority to complement
the existing nontariff authority was unrealistic since
it had been unsuccessfully trying to obtain such
authority for some time.

From February to May, at the request of the USTR, the
U.S. International Trade Commission (ITC) prepared a
study on the FTA's impact on the United States. Most
Congressional action was set aside until the study was
completed. During this period, there was a great deal
of doubt as to whether a trade bill would pass before
the election.[32] Because the domestic political pressures are usually against trade liberalizing legislation, a trade bill must have sufficient measures that
appeal to Congress to overcome these disincentives. As
a result, trade legislation has been traditionally
difficult to pass through Congress. By the end of July,
the Congress had almost run out of time to pass
legislation granting tariff negotiating authority to the
President. Congress would recess for the month of
August and then go out of session in October for the
election recess.

---

[32]Alexander Platt, former Associate General
Counsel, Office of the U.S. Trade Representative,
interview by the author, Washington D.C.,
March 22, 1986.

On April 5, 1984 a bill was introduced by Congressman
Thomas Downey (D-California) which, in essence, gave the
President full authority, with almost no limitations, to
proclaim all tariff reductions and nontariff agreements
negotiated with Israel without Congressional review.[33]
This bill was strongly supported by the pro-Israel
lobby, but was not accepted by the Administration for
several reasons. The Administration did not want
legislation that was limited solely to Israel, but
rather wanted legislation that could be used to negotiate free trade areas with other countries. The
Administration also believed that given the general
desire of Congress to circumscribe the power of the
President in the negotiation of trade agreements, the
chance of the Downey bill ever passing Congress was
extremely slim.[34]

The Downey bill was amended in the House Ways and Means
Trade Subcommittee and in the full Committee. These
amendments served principally to circumscribe the
President's negotiating authority by requiring that the
agreement be brought back to the Congress for implementation. On October 3, 1984, the amended bill passed
the full House and was incorporated into an omnibus

---

[33]Ibid., p. 15.

[34]Platt interview, March 22, 1986.

trade bill, which would become the Tariff and Trade Act of 1984.

In the Senate, a bill was introduced by Senator Robert Dole (R-Kansas) which provided the President with authority to negotiate free trade areas with both Israel and Canada. This bill contained an additional clause which provided the President with authority to negotiate FTA's with other countries after consulting with, and obtaining approval from, the House Ways and Means and the Senate Finance Committees. This bill was incorporated into the Senate version of the omnibus trade bill, which passed the full Senate on September 20, 1984.

On October 4, the Senate and House versions of the omnibus trade bill were sent to the Conference Committee, and on October 9, 1984 both the House and Senate approved the Conference report. On October 30, 1984, the President signed into law the Tariff and Trade Act of 1984 which contained authority to negotiate the FTA with Israel.

The final legislation combined the existing section 102 authority for nontariff barriers with authority to negotiate tariff reductions, with the requirement that

FTA negotiated with Israel be submitted for implementation by Congress under the fast-track procedure.[35]
Although the Administration had requested broader negotiating authority that would have given empowered it to
negotiate free trade areas with countries other than
Israel, the final legislation provided this authority
only under specific conditions. These conditions were,
first that the country requests the negotiations, and
second, that the House Ways and Means and Senate Finance
committees do not disapprove of such negotiations.[36]

Congressional Influence on the Negotiations
While Congress did not grant formal negotiating authority until October, the Executive branch had been
negotiating with Israel on the FTA since January 1984.
The Administration was in close touch with Congress
throughout, in order to ensure that the negotiations
were **proceeding** in a direction that would receive the
necessary Congressional support. During this period,
Congress held numerous hearings on the free trade area
and was a constant source of pressure on the Administration to protect a long list of "sensitive industries."

---

[35]Platt, "Free Trade with Israel," p. 11.

[36]The Trade and Tariff Act of 1984, section 401.

Before the ITC report was published, Congress tried to pressure the Administration to eliminate Israel's agriculture subsidies. The pressure came primarily from Senator Pete Wilson (R-California), Congressman William Thomas (R-California), who is on the House Ways and Means Committee, and the rest of the California delegation. A Congressional delegation travelled to Israel in August 1984 to visit farms and factories and meet with Israeli industry leaders. The primary purpose of their visit was examine Israel's production and export capability in sectors that concerned the Congress.[37] During this visit, Israeli officials spent a considerable amount of time discussing the subsidy issue, explaining that their agricultural subsidies were actually quite low, and were primarily for irrigation and for farms in desert areas. Congress was also swayed by the Administration's argument that it was unrealistic to ask Israel to eliminate its agricultural subsidies as long as the U.S. U.S. still maintained its own. In addition, the Administration pointed out that Israel was still subject to U.S. countervailing duty laws, to which U.S. farmers had recourse in the case of injury.

---

[37]Thelma Aske, Staff member, House Ways and Means Committee, Subcommittee on Trade, interview by author, Washington D.C., January 18, 1985.

Congressional pressure on the agricultural subsidy issue
was mitigated by late summer, and once the ITC published
its findings in May 1984, Congressional pressure shifted
to excluding the items contained in the ITC list.

Congress, and particularly Congressmen from districts
producing products the ITC had declared sensitive,
exerted tremendous pressure on the Executive branch to
exclude from the agreement the items the ITC had
determined were sensitive. Certain members of Congress
even called for the FTA to have the same exclusions list
as the Caribbean Basin Initiative.[38] The issue of how
to handle the ITC list would be one of the most conten-
tious issues within the U.S. government during the
course of the FTA negotiations. The fight to exclude
the ITC list was headed by the California delegation on
behalf of the agricultural community, and Congressman
Beryl Anthony (D-Arkansas) on behalf of the bromine producers.

Israeli negotiators viewed the inclusion of the items on
the ITC list in the agreement was a critical requirement
in order for Israel to agree to the agreement, and

---

[38]Mary Jane Wignot, Staff Director, House Ways and
Means Subcommittee on Trade, interview by author,
Washington D.C., March 14, 1985. CBI and GSP have a
series of product exclusions, including textiles and a
variety of other sensitive products.

threatened to walk out of the negotiations unless a final date for eliminating tariffs on the products identified by the ITC was agreed upon.[39] USTR Brock and Israel's Minister of Trade, however, had already made a committment to each other that neither side would have any exclusions, as a precondition to negotiating the agreement. The Administration also believed that the agreement should not have any exclusions in order for it to be considered GATT-legal.[40] It was at this point that USTR Brock promised the Israelis that all the ITC items would be included in the FTA by January 1, 1995.

In order to win the support of Congress, U.S. Trade Representative Brock gave the Congress a commitment that the items identified by the ITC as sensitive would be put in a separate category with tariffs frozen at their current levels for ten years.[41] The issue as to whether these items would be subsequently included in the agreement was left unclarified, with Brock promising

---

[39]Shmuel Cohen, Assistant to the Deputy Director General for Foreign Trade, Ministry of Agriculture, interview by author, Tel Aviv, May 16, 1985.

[40]According to GATT Article XXIV, section 8(b), "A free trade area shall be understood to mean a group of two or more customs territories in which the duties and other restrictive regulations of commerce ... are eliminated on all substantially all the trade between the two constituent territories..."

[41]Adams interview, July 31, 1985.

inclusion to the Israelis and many Congressmen assuming the frozen items would be excluded from the agreement.[42] This issue was, in fact, never clarified until Congress debated the authorization for negotiation of the FTA in October.[43]

The House Ways and Means and the Senate Finance Committees disagreed on how the ITC list should be handled. The Senate wanted USTR to obtain Congressional approval in order to eliminate the tariffs on any items on the frozen list. The House rejected this viewpoint, asserting that such approval could potentially put the Administration in the position of violating the GATT if

---

[42]Government officials involved in the negotiations said that Brock knew that the Israel would only agree to an agreement with no exclusions, and that this was the only way that the agreement would qualify as a free trade area under the GATT (a necessary condition if the FTA was to be a precedent for other FTAs). He hoped that by promising key Congressmen special treatment on products of interest, Congressional support of the agreement would be maintained until negotiation of the entire agreement had been completed. Since the bill had been submitted on a no ammendment basis, with only an up or down vote, Brock hoped that Congress would pass the bill when faced with a completed agreement.

[43]The Senate originally wanted the bill to require that the Congress have an opportunity to consider the liberalization of the frozen list before the automatic elimination of tariffs on those items. The final agreement specifies obtaining USITC advice after five years. If any of the products are no longer deemed sensitive, congressional approval would be needed for an accelerated duty reduction. For the other items, the form of the final duty elimination was not spelled out in the bill, although a commitment was made to eliminate all duties by 1/1/95.

the tariffs were never eliminated. The eventual
decision was that all the tariffs would be eliminated
after ten years, with a compromise solution to freeze
tariffs for five years and seek ITC advice at that
time. If based on that advice, USTR wishes to eliminate
the tariffs before the ten-year mark, Congressional
approval would be required.

The second issue that the Administration juggled with
Congress until late in the negotiation process was
whether GSP eligibility superceded the FTA tariff
elimination. The Administration never clarified that
Israel would still be eligible for duty-free treatment
under the GSP program until 1995. At that time the FTA
would be completely phased in. Thus, for items in the
later stages of tariff elimination which were eligible
for GSP (such as jewelry) duty-free treatment would
still apply. This upset Congressional members who
thought placing certain items in the later tranches
would protect them for a longer period of time-- despite
the fact that they had been entering the U.S. under the
GSP program. From the Administration's point of view,
it was untenable to ask Israel to give up existing GSP
benefits which were already in effect.

Even after Congress passed the authorizing legislation

in October, it was in constant consultation with the
Administration throughout the remainder of the negotiations. The official negotiations were concluded at
the end of January, with the last official negotiation
session, devoted to textiles, taking place on January
23, 1985. On March 7, 1985, both countries initialed
the FTA agreement.[44]

Under the "fast-track" provisions, a bill cannot be
amended after it is officially introduced. Therefore,
the FTA was unofficially given to the House Ways and
Means and Senate Finance Committees before it was
officially introduced for implementation. During March
1985, each committee held a "non-markup" of the bill and
made "unofficial" changes in preparation for the final
version of the agreement.[45] A "non-conference" committee meeting was then held to resolve differences
between the two marked-up bills.[46] The bill was then
given back to the Administration in a form that the
committees believed Congress would be comfortable

---

[44]Initialing of an agreement is an official
indication that negotiations have been completed, but
there are technical changes that need to be made before
formal signing.

[45]Wignot interview, January 14, 1985.

[46]Since Congress had been so involved throughout
the negotiation, and had the opportunity to have its
concerns resolved earlier in the process, few changes
were made at this time.

passing without amending. It was only at this point
that the Administration officially submitted the bill to
Congress.

The "Agreement on the Establishment of a Free Trade Area
between the Government of the United States of America
and the Government of Israel" was signed by both trade
ministers on April 22, 1985. The United States Free
Trade Area Implementation Act of 1985 was passed by both
houses of Congress and became Public Law 99-47 on June
11, 1985. Because of the textile dispute,[47] which broke
out during this period, Israel initially stated that it
would not sign the agreement until the dispute was
resolved. As the summer wore on, U.S. officials became
concerned about whether the September 1, 1985 implementation date for tariffs would be met. Although the
textile dispute was still unresolved, the Israeli
Cabinet voted to implement the agreement on August 18,
1985. On August 19, 1985, the GATT was notified and the
U.S.-Israel Free Trade Area Agreement entered into
force.

-----

[47]See chapter V for a complete discussion of the
textile dispute.

D.   The ITC Report

While the ITC is a nonpolitical agency with a mandate to
provide both the Executive branch and the Congress with
impartial information, the report it produced on the
domestic impact of the FTA was used by both branches of
government to accomplish certain political ends.
Despite the fact that the ITC's recommendations were
advisory rather than obligatory, once the report was
completed, it became a bible. The items identified in
the ITC report were thereafter placed in a special
category of tariff elimination and treated differently;
no items were added or subtracted from the list after it
was released. The main reason for this was political
expediency. USTR Brock and other administration
officials used the list as a bargaining chip to prevent
the Congress from legislating permanent exclusions to
the FTA. By saying that they would take care of the
items identified by the ITC, the administration was able
to show that they were taking care of items "officially"
identified as sensitive, and thereby fend off pressures
for special treatment of additional items of interest to
Congress but not identified in the ITC report.

Similarly, Congress, insisted that the items identified by ITC be placed in a separate category so that it could report to its constituents that it had taken care of those items "officially" identified as sensitive. Thus, the ITC report became an extremely important document in the course of the FTA negotiations, taking on a role which was much larger than its original intent. This section will describe and analyze the report issued by the ITC.

On January 30, 1984, the U.S. International Trade Commission (ITC) received a request for an investigation under section 332(g) of the Tariff Act of 1930[48] from the USTR concerning "the probable effect of providing duty-free treatment for imports from Israel on industries in the United States providing like or directly competitive articles and on consumers."[49] The ITC initiated its investigation on February 8, 1984, with a projected completion date of May 30, 1984. The ITC held public hearings on April 10 and 11 during which all

---

[48]A request for investigation by the USITC under section 332(g) of the Tariff Act of 1930 (19 U.S.C. 1332(g)) can be filed by U.S. government or industry.

[49]William E. Brock, former U.S. Trade Representative, letter to U.S. International Trade Commission Chairman Alfred Eckes, January 25, 1984. Letter in possession of the U.S. International Trade Commission, Washington D.C.

interested parties were able to appear and state their view on the impact of the proposed free trade area in general, or its impact on a particular sector.

The following items were identified as sensitive with regard to imports from Israel by the ITC report, comprising a total of 43 Tariff Schedule of the U.S.A. (TSUSA) items: processed tomatoes, olives, citrus fruit juices, fresh cut roses, dried onion and garlic, certain bromine products, and certain gold jewelry. Examining the seven categories of items identified raises questions about how the ITC decided that these products were "sensitive." Of these products, processed tomatoes are by far Israel's largest export to the U.S. ($20.6 million in 1983); they make up 21% of total U.S processed tomato imports in 1983, although only 3% of apparent U.S. consumption. The fact that Israel is the leading supplier of processed tomato products to the U.S., combined with a recession in the U.S. industry and growth in the Israeli industry, made this product the most logical item for the ITC to have included on its list.

Israel ranks third among suppliers of olive imports to the U.S. market, with $1.7 million in imports in 1983 or 2% of olive imports. The California olive industry has

been declining in recent years and faces stiff import
competition from a number of Mediterranean countries,
primarily Greece and Spain. Once again, this was a
situation where the U.S. olive industry was under
substantial import pressure and Israel was a competitive
and growing supplier. Yet Israel is a much more minor
supplier of olives-- in dollars and market share-- than
of processed tomatoes.

Although Colombia accounts for the bulk of U.S. flower
imports, Israel is the second largest exporter of fresh
cut roses to U.S. In 1983, Colombian exports to the
U.S. of fresh cut roses amounted to $26 million as
compared to Israel's $441,000.[50] In 1982, imports of
cut roses from Israel made up only 1.6% of total
U.S. imports and .2% of consumption. Because of the
import sensitivity of the domestic rose industry, roses
were determined ineligible for duty-free status under
the GSP program. The industry has brought two escape
clause cases to the ITC, and has filed two countervailing duty cases against cut flowers from Israel.

Israel does not export any dehydrated garlic and onion

---

[50]U.S. International Trade Commission, "Fresh Cut
Roses from Colombia: Determination of the Commission,"
Investigation No. 731-TA-148 (preliminary), Washington
D.C., November 1983, Table 9.

products, garlic or onion flour, or tomato flour to the
U.S. Dehydrated onion and garlic, and onion and garlic
powder have tariffs ranging from 28.8% to 35%, and the
ITC concluded that with such a large reduction in
tariffs, Israeli dehydrators would have an incentive to
shift their production lines to these products.
Although the dehydrated garlic and onion industry was
successful in keeping its products from being eligible
for duty-free treatment under the GSP program, total
imports amounted to only 2.4% of domestic consumption in
1982.

The key item of concern in the category of citrus juices
was frozen concentrate orange juice (FCOJ). The
U.S. industry generally buys juice from other countries
to blend with its own. Although U.S. imports of FCOJ
from Israel in 1982 were negligible, Israel has been a
supplier in the past, depending on the yield of the
U.S. citrus crop. For the past few years, Brazil has
been by far the most competitive exporter of FCOJ to the
U.S. Since Israel is a large exporter of FCOJ to
Western Europe, the primary concern of the ITC was that
the removal of an ad valorem equivalent tariff of 43.5%
would enable Israel to become a competitive exporter to
the U.S. The second concern was that Israel could
import FCOJ from Brazil, blend it with Israeli juice and

then reexport it to the U.S. at a lower cost than the
equivalent amount shipped directly to the U.S. from
Brazil with the existing duty.

Israel is the second largest manufacturer of bromine
compounds in the world and is the largest exporter of
bromine products to the U.S., making up 71% of U.S. imports in 1982 and 5% of apparent consumption. The
largest component of the bromine industry, ethylene
dibromide, is an ingredient of leaded gas, which the EPA
is advocating phasing out because of its toxicity.
Production of other bromine compounds used in pesticides
is declining for similar environmental reasons.
Industry growth is now led by well-drilling fluids and
flame retardants. Of the twenty-eight TSUSA numbers for
bromine compounds, ten TSUSA numbers were chosen as
importsensitive by the ITC.

The final item identified as sensitive in the ITC report
was gold jewelry. U.S. imports of gold jewelry have
been steadily growing, accounting for 67% of consumption
in 1982. Italy is by far the largest supplier of gold
jewelry imports into the U.S., with 52% of the market in
1983. Israel trailed as the second largest supplier
with 8% of the U.S. market in 1983. These gains have
come at a time when domestic manufacturers have been

reporting significant drops in production. While almost
all of Israel's jewelry exports enter the U.S. duty free
under the GSP program, Israel's exports in this sector
have been very close to the GSP competitive-needs limit
for some time. In fact, in 1981, the ITC disaggregated
the tariff item 74010 into items 74013 (gold necklaces)
and 74014 (jewelry of precious metals except gold).
This division preserved Israel's access to the GSP
program in this commodity. Without it, Israel's exports
of gold necklaces would have exceeded the competitive
needs limit in 1980. Because of this, the ITC was
familiar with the case of gold jewelry imports from
Israel.

Examining at the products identified by the ITC in its
report, in none of the product categories do exports
from Israel comprise more than 8% of apparent U.S. consumption. If it is assumed, however, that certain
industries facing increased import competition may need
more time to adjust to duty-free imports from Israel,
certainly processed tomato products and perhaps bromine
products, would be among this category of industries.
In the case of gold jewelry, the reasoning behind
identifying it as sensitive in terms of tariff is weak
since almost all gold jewelry already enters the U.S.
duty-free under GSP. The ITC report acknowledges that

an increase in gold jewelry imports from Israel is
unlikely in the short run since the product is already
entering duty-free, but states that duty elimination
under the FTA would remove the uncertainty about the
future of the GSP program and allow Israeli companies to
commit themselves to increasing production. While this
is true in the longer run, it does not seem to be
sufficient cause for the ITC to have identified gold
jewelry.

Although the elimination of the tariff on FCOJ may lead
Israel to increase its exports of FCOJ to the U.S.,
Israel has been a very minor player in the U.S. FCOJ
market to date. The issue of transshipment from Brazil
was addressed when the Congress insisted that the
Administration use the stringent rules of origin that
were used in the Caribbean Basin Initiative program. No
problem has surfaced with transshipment in the IsraelEEC
arrangement, and because Israel is a small country with
well- known production levels, any unusually large
shipment from Israel would be noticeable.

The ITC's identification of dehydrated garlic and
onions, as well as onion, garlic, and tomato flour is
difficult to understand, given the fact that Israel does
not currently export any to the U.S. While it may be

true that Israel could start to produce these products, this alone seems like weak ground for the products to have been identified by the ITC.

Although Israel is the second largest exporter of cut roses to the U.S., its exports amount to only 0.2% of domestic consumption. The U.S. cut rose industry is experiencing problems due to imports from Colombia, not Israel. Once again, the ITC is familiar with this industry because the industry was removed from the GSP program and because of the two countervailing duty (CVD) cases filed against Israel. The fact that CVD cases were filed, however, should not necessarily play a role in the ITC decision with regard to the FTA. In fact, the countervailing duty of 22.6% imposed against Israel is by far a more significant deterrent to imports than the 8% duty on cut roses.

While the three major U.S. companies that dominate the bromine industry seem to be financially sound, almost the entire industry is located in two counties in Arkansas which are among the most indigent in the U.S. The bromine industry has thus traditionally been viewed as a labor adjustment problem. While it is clear that certain segments of the bromine industry are shrinking, it is not clear why the ITC selected the ten bromine

items chosen. The ten items chosen-- well-drilling
fluids and flame retardants-- are considered to be the
future of the industry, not the segments of the industry
that are currently in decline and experiencing the bulk
of the import competition. A justification used by the
ITC in its explanation of which bromine items it singled
out, was that fourteen out of the eighteen remaining
items not identified are eligible for dutyfree treatment
under the GSP program, and therefore imports would not
really be affected by tariff elimination. This seems to
contradict the argument the ITC used for identifying
gold jewelry as sensitive despite the fact that it is
eligible for GSP.

A number of Administration officials expressed the view
that the ITC should not have treated textile products as
one item, but rather should have looked more closely at
individual items.[51] While clearly Israel is a very
minor exporter to the U.S. in the textile sector as a
whole, in certain small segments, such as knit wear, it
is slightly more significant. Most likely, the ITC did
not do this because it would have been politically
difficult to identify a only a few textile products, and
the overall impact of Israeli imports in that sector is
negligible. Furthermore, the ITC knew that the com-

---

[51]Adams interview, July 31, 1985.

prehensive system of quotas protecting the textile industry would remain in place, providing guaranteed protection from any increases in imports from Israel in that sector.

Thus, despite the problems with the ITC report, it became a critical document in the negotiations because having a list of items "officially" identified as sensitive to imports from Israel was politically expedient to both the Administration and the Congress.

E.   The Role of Pressure Groups

Pressure groups are an integral part of the trade policy process, informing and influencing all branches of government. Congress is particularly vulnerable to pressure from constituent groups, typically industry groups[52] and labor unions, because it relies on constituent votes to remain in office. While officials in the Executive branch are not dependent on constituent groups for votes to remain in office, workers in government agencies are nonetheless favorably disposed to the

---

[52]The term industry groups refers here to groups representing both manufacturing and agricultural sectors.

industry or labor groups that the agencies represent.[53]
Although the ITC is an independent quasi-judicial
agency, it too is subject to pressure from industry
groups to the extent that it is affected by which groups
present their cases to the ITC and how well those cases
are presented.

Most industry groups today are well informed on the
nuances of trade policy issues and are ready to be
actively involved. Even in a case like the FTA, where
the expected economic effects on the U.S. are negligible, a significant amount of opposition was expressed
by the domestic industry. Because of the nature of the
lobbying process, relatively small groups can often
exert a disproportionate effect. Even the smallest trade
association can have a representative located in
Washington D.C., whose sole responsibility is to lobby
Congress on issues that pertain to that association.
Since they already have a representative following
Congress, no additional cost is involved for that
person, or group of persons, to lobby Congress on any
issue of concern. Thus, trade legislation usually
brings a scrambling of trade associations, each trying
to exert influence on the process. Manufacturers and

---

[53]For a discussion of the effect of pressure groups
on civil servants, see Baldwin, The Political Economy of
U.S. Import Policy.

unions opposed to trade liberalization, or in favor of
increased protectionism, are generally much more
cohesive and better organized than the importers and
exporters that favor trade liberalization, or other
groups that favor free trade.[54] U.S. exporters to
Israel did not play an active role in the FTA negotiations since the Israeli market is small and the perceived opportunities by U.S. exporters insubstantial.

Because international trade is interwoven with foreign
policy, there were also groups whose concern about the
FTA was based on its foreign policy implications. On
one side, Arab organizations opposed the FTA because
they feared a free trade area with Israel would harm
U.S. relations with Arab nations. On the other side
stood the American Israel Public Affairs Committee
(AIPAC), which believed that the FTA would be a key step
in cementing political relations between the U.S. and
Israel. AIPAC took its lobbying experience and constituency and began working on the FTA. To counter the
economic objections to the FTA, AIPAC emphasized the
economic benefits of the FTA for the U.S. In selling
the FTA to the Congress, AIPAC promoted it as a "unique
experiment for the U.S., under highly favorable con-

---

[54]See chapter II for a literature review of the
role of pressure groups in trade policy.

ditions and with very limited risks."[55] Secondarily,
AIPAC argued that the FTA would help strengthen Israel's
economy which would reduce its dependence on U.S.
foreign aid and enhance its value to the U.S. as a
stable, democratic ally in the Middle East.

Before a bill on the FTA was even introduced, Congress
was heavily lobbied by a wide range of domestic manufacturers. Congressional pressure on the Administration
often starts in the form of a letter from a Congressman
on behalf of a constituent who has written a letter of
concern. Letters from constituents and Congressmen
began pouring into the USTR's office shortly after
negotiations on the free trade area began, and continued
to arrive by the thousands throughout the course of the
negotiations. Letters of particular concern to the
Administration were those from members sitting on either
the House Ways and Means Committee or the Senate Finance
Committee, the two committees with jurisdiction on the
FTA legislation. For example, in his March 7, 1984
letter to USTR Brock, Congressman Beryl Anthony
(D-Arkansas) explains that his district in Arkansas
produces over 85% of the bromine produced in the United

---

[55]Peggy Blair, "A U.S.-Israel Free Trade Area: How
Both Sides Gain," American Israel Public Affairs
Committee papers on U.S.-Israel relations, No.9,
Washington D.C., 1984, p. 2.

States. His letter goes on to say that the domestic
industry has been experiencing a range of problems and
asks that bromine be excluded from the FTA.[56] Brock
responded by acknowledging the concern and added that he
was waiting to see the results of the ITC report.

Generally, domestic manufacturers expressed support for
the concept of a U.S.-Israel FTA, but requested that
their product be granted a special exemption from having
its tariff eliminated. Among agricultural groups, the
American processed tomato, citrus juice, avocados,
dehydrated garlic and onion, olive, and cut roses
industries all submitted requests to both branches of
government for exclusion of their products from the
FTA. Among industry groups, exclusion requests came
from the footwear, textile and apparel, gold jewelry,
and bromine industries. Even though Israeli exports of
these products to the U.S. are not significant, these
industries argued that they were import sensitive and
should be excluded from the FTA. These industry
associations testified at the interagency Trade Policy
Committee hearings and at the U.S. International Trade

---

[56]Beryl Anthony, Congressman, letter to U.S. Trade
Representative William E. Brock, March 7, 1984. Letter
in possession of the Office of the U.S. Trade Representative, Washington D.C.

Commission, before testifying before Congress.[57]

The second set of groups opposed to the FTA did so on
grounds that it would set a dangerous precedent. The
AFL-CIO testified in opposition to the FTA, stating that
at a time when the U.S. is experiencing a large mer-
chandise trade deficit and a rapidly increasing volume
of imports, reduction of U.S. tariff and nontariff
barriers "places an additional burden on American
workers."[58] The U.S. textile manufacturers claimed that
their real worry was not Israel per se, but that the
U.S.-Israel FTA will set a precedent that may lead to a
proliferation of free trade areas. The AFL-CIO and
domestic manufacturers were particularly concerned about
the possibility of free trade areas with low-wage
countries such as Korea and Taiwan, resulting in a flood
of imports into the U.S.

The textile industry actively lobbied for exclusion from
the FTA. Considered one of the most powerful industrial

---

[57]U.S. International Trade Commission, "Probable
Economic Effect of Providing Duty-Free Treatment for
Imports from Israel," Investigation No.332-180,
Washington D.C., May 1984.

[58]Stephen Koplan, AFL-CIO, testimony to the House
Ways and Means Committee, Subcommittee on Trade,
"Proposed United States-Israel Free Trade Area," Ninety-
Eighth Congress, Second Session, Washington D.C., May
22, 1984, p. 105.

lobbies in the U.S., the textile industry has the strong allegiance from many southern Congressmen who represent the states where a majority of the industry is located. These Congressmen have historically voted an unparalleled degree of protection for the industry. The textile sector is the most heavily protected industrial sector in the U.S., protected by high tariffs and the Multifiber Arrangement, an international system of allocated bilateral quotas governing textile and apparel imports into the United States. The textile manufacturers claimed that textiles should be excluded from the FTA since they had been excluded from other U.S. preference arrangements such as GSP and the Caribbean Basin Initiative. They wanted to reinforce the notion that textiles need to be given special treatment and routinely excluded from liberalizing agreements.

Even though Israel's share of total U.S. textile and apparel imports in 1982 amounted to only 0.2% or $17.4 million,[59] the U.S. industry insisted the sector be excluded from the FTA. It was concerned about the principle that concessions should not be made in textiles, and feared that the FTA would set a precedent for future bilateral agreements with more significant textile

---

[59]U.S. Department of Commerce, Import Monthly, series 145, Washington D.C., 1983.

exporting countries. The industry was also concerned about the potential growth of Israel's textile exports to the U.S. Two key Congressmen on the House Ways and Means Committee who fought for the exclusion of the textile sector from the FTA were Congressman Ed Jenkins (D-Georgia), who is also Chairman of the Textile Caucus, and Carroll Campbell (R-South Carolina), a Congressman who has traditionally championed the cause of the footwear and textile industries.[60]

As in the negotiation of other trade agreements, the industries that made their case known were generally the ones who received "special attention" in the course of the negotiation. The list of items identified as sensitive by the ITC has a strong correlation with the list of industries that testified at its hearings. Senators Bumpers (D-Arkansas), and Pryor (D-Arkansas) and, Congressman Anthony (D-Arkansas), as well as the Governor of Arkansas appeared at the hearings on behalf of the bromine industry. In addition, two bromine industry representatives testified. The Vice President of the American Dehydrated Onion and Garlic Association testified, as did the President of the California Olive Growers Association. Roses Incorporated gave testimony in favor of rose growers and the Sun Garden

---

[60]Wignot interview, January 14, 1985.

Packing Company testified on behalf of processed tomatoes and apricots. Congressman Delbert Latta (R-Ohio) and a total of nine industry representatives testified on behalf of processed tomato producers. Industries which presented testimony but whose products were not identified by the ITC as sensitive items were the dairy industry, peppers and pimentos, avocadoes, the American Textile Manufacturing Association, leather footwear and luggage, and nonrubber footwear.

Only one product, gold jewelry, which the ITC found to be import sensitive, had only a written submission and no oral testimony before the ITC. Production of gold jewelry is predominantly located in Rhode Island. Senator Chaffee (R-Rhode Island) a member of the Trade Subcommittee of the Senate Finance Committee, was on good terms with USTR Brock and had staunchly advocated special treatment for the industry on previous occasions.

Almost all the industry representatives who testified at the ITC subsequently testified at the hearings held by the Trade Policy SubCommittee later in the month of April, and then at the Congressional hearings held in May and June. A key factor in whether an industry's requests were accepted in the FTA negotiations was how early in the process they were voiced, and whether they appeared at the ITC hearings. As a number of individuals involved in the negotiations commented, the products that were "taken care of" were the ones that had their case presented by February or March of 1984.[61]

The House Ways and Means Subcommittee on Trade held hearings on the proposed U.S.-Israel Free Trade Area on May 22, and June 13 and 14, 1984. Representatives from the citrus, olives, processed tomato, roses, bromine, dried onion and garlic, bromine, and textile industries were present. Five members of Congress testified; Senator David Pryor (D-Arkansas) and Congressman Beryl Anthony (D-Arkansas) on behalf of the bromine industry, Congressmen William Thomas (R-California) and Norman Shumway (R-California) on behalf of citrus, tomatoes, and olives, and Congresswoman Barbara Vucanovich (R-Nevada) on behalf of the dried onion and garlic industry.

The dairy industry's primary concern was to make sure that the elimination of nontariff barriers under the FTA not extend to the dairy quotas under section 22 of the

---

[61]Platt interview, March 22, 1986.

Agricultural Adjustment Act.[62] Since U.S. quotas on the
dairy sector are quite stringent, the elimination of
tariffs alone would not have a significant impact on
imports. Although Israel requested a relaxation of the
Section 22 quotas as part of the FTA, this was not
granted, primarily due to the insistence of the Department of Agriculture and the Congress.[63] The ITC did not
identify the dairy industry in its report because it
realized that the quotas protecting the industry would
remain in place. Consequently, dairy products ended up
in the five-year category with respect to tariff elimination.

Although the avocado growers submitted testimony to the
ITC (they did not testify in person) and testified
before Congress, avocadoes were not identified as
sensitive by the ITC. Due to stringent USDA phyto-
sanitary regulations, no avocadoes are imported into the
United States.

In addition to their concern about the impact of the FTA

------

[62]R.F. Anderson, Executive Director, American
Butter Institute-National Cheese Institute, Inc.,
written statement to the House Ways and Means Subcommittee on Trade, June 14, 1984, p. 570.

[63]Dewey Pritchard, International Economist,
U.S. Department of Agriculture, interview by author,
Washington D.C., March 25, 1986.

on imports into the U.S., the fruit and vegetable
producers that testified before Congress also stressed
the fact that they could not anticipate any export
benefit from an FTA with Israel. This was confirmed by
the testimony of the Deputy Undersecretary of the USDA
Alan Tracy who stated that the FTA would primarily
benefit U.S. exports of industrial products, while
U.S. imports of horticultural[64] products from Israel
would be expected to increase.[65] Tracy's testimony also
raised concerns about Israel's agricultural subsidies,
saying that "the benefits of duty elimination should not
accrue to subsidized exports."[66] Agricultural producers
also argued that when Spain and Portugal, two major
fruit and vegetable producers, join the European
Economic Community in a few of years, Israel's exports
to the EEC will be displaced and it will be forced to
divert its agricultural exports to the United States.

American producers stressed that Israel's production of
fruits, vegetables, and flowers is heavily subsidized by

---

[64]The term "horticultural" is used to refer to the
cultivation of fruits, vegetables, and flowers, as
opposed to "agricultural" which also includes grains and
livestock.

[65]Alan Tracy, Deputy Undersecretary of Agriculture,
testimony to the House Ways and Means Subcommittee on
Trade, June 14, 1984, p.399.

[66]Ibid.

the Israeli government, and that the U.S. had a $30
million deficit in horticultural trade with Israel in
1982.[67]   Taking a somewhat broader perspective,
however, all U.S. agricultural exports to Israel
totalled close to $400 million in 1983 (this includes
grains, the primary U.S. agricultural export to Israel)
and have consistently been five to six times as great as
U.S. agricultural imports from Israel.

In general, the agriculture sector provided the
quickest, most sophisticated response to the FTA
negotiations. They gave detailed information to both
the ITC and the Congress, and testified at hearings held
by the ITC, Congress, and the TPSC. It can be hypothesized that the agricultural community has traditionally been more oriented towards international trade
than the manufacturing sector. It was, therefore,
better equipped to provide specific information about
which products Israel had capabilities in and the which
areas their exports to the U.S. would be likely to
increase as a result of the FTA. USDA commodity
specialists work very closely with the agricultural
trade associations and were quick to assess the
potential impact of the FTA on each product very early

---

[67]W. Glenn Tussey, Assistant Director, American
Farm Bureau Federation, testimony to the House Ways and
Means Subcommittee on Trade, June 13, 1984, p. 328.

in the negotiation process. By February 1984 they had
determined which products were potentially sensitive to
imports from Israel.[68]

By contrast, the textile and apparel industry argued for
exclusion of the entire sector from the FTA. When it
became clear that the Administration was committed to an
agreement with no exclusions, the textile industry was
unable to provide information to the government about
those products which were the most sensitive to imports
from Israel. Perhaps, had the textile industry pushed
the exclusion of one or two specific products, those
items would have been identified by the ITC. Still
another possibility is that the textile industry did not
feel the need to provide specific information to the
government since it knew it was protected by the system
of managed trade in that sector. The industry was
confident that if textile imports from Israel increased,
the Department of Commerce would set a quota to limit
imports of that product. It is also possible that the
textile industry was confident enough about its political power in Congress to know that the entire industry
sector would be protected in the negotiations. In fact,
out of 3,845 textile tariff items in the negotiation,
only 223 items had any imports from Israel, yet over 80%

---

[68]Pritchard interview, March 25, 1985.

of textile items were placed in the third tranche in the final agreement.

F.   Summary

Several themes recur throughout the U.S. policy process that led to the negotiation and implementation of the U.S.-Israel FTA. First, because of their constitutionally mandated partnership, the Executive branch was forced to work closely with the Congress throughout the FTA negotiations to craft an agreement that the Congress could sell to its constituents and that the President could sell to the Israeli negotiators. The Executive branch started its discussions with Congress immediately after a decision to negotiate an FTA was reached with Israel. These discussions began by examining which legislative vehicle should be used to grant the President authority to negotiate. The Administration then proceeded to simultaneous discussions with both the Congress and with Israel on what shape the agreement should take.

The second theme has to do with how the Administration used Congressional pressure to extract concessions from Israel. For instance, because of Congressional pressure, the Administration was able to tell Israel

that the ITC freeze list was completely non-negotiable,
and that Israel was fortunate that the Administration
had successfully gotten agreement from the Congress not
to exclude the entire list from the FTA. On the other
hand, the Administration was also able to pressure the
Congress by first making certain concessions to Israel,
such as maintaining GSP eligibility for items placed in
later tranches, and then telling the Congress that
Israel would not agree to the agreement if these
concessions were taken back.

The third theme shows how the ITC report became a focal
point in the discussions between the Executive branch
and the Congress and in the negotiations. Because of
the political expediency offered by having an official
document which identified a group of industries as
import sensitive, the recommendations of the ITC became
set in stone.

The final theme focuses on the influence of pressure
groups throughout the entire FTA process. Industry
groups began contacting Congressmen from the very
earliest point in the process, and continued through the
negotiations. In turn, Congress applied pressure on the
Administration to deal with the issues raised by its
constituency, such as agriculture subsidies and the

elimination of sensitive items from the agreement.
Pressure groups also affected decision making in the
Executive branch and the ITC. Both the Administration
and the Congress were positively predisposed to pressure
they received from currently protected industries, such
as textiles and agriculture, which were concerned about
maintaining their protected status in the context of the
FTA. Other individual industries that applied enough
political pressure were also successful in obtaining
special treatment in the FTA negotiations. Looking at
the ITC report, a correlation exists between the
industries that testified before the ITC, the TPSC and
the Congress, and the items the ITC identified as sensitive. The Administration also made an effort to
protect the textile industry, despite the fact that the
ITC report stated that the impact on the domestic
textile industry resulting from Israeli imports would be
negligible. In fact, of the last two tranches of the
agreement, the third is composed of primarily of textile
items, and the fourth is entirely composed of the ITC
list.

APPENDIX I

CONGRESSIONAL TRADE SUBCOMMITTEE MEMBERSHIP

(During the Ninety-Eighth Congress)

House Ways and Means, Subcommittee on Trade

Sam Gibbons,(D-Florida) (Chairman)
Dan Rostenkowski, (D-Illinois)
James Jones, (D-Oklahoma)
Ed Jenkins, (D-Georgia)
Thomas Downey, (D-California)
Don Pease, (D-Ohio)
Kent Hance, (D-Texas)
Cecil Heftel, (D-Hawaii)
Marty Russo, (D-Illinois)

Guy Vander Jagt, (R-Michigan)
Bill Archer, (R-Texas)
Bill Frenzel, (R-Minnesota)
Richard Schulze, (R-Pennsylvania)
Phillip Crane, (R-Illinois)

Senate Finance, Subcommittee on Trade

Jack Danforth, (R-Missouri) (Chairman)
John Chaffee, (R-Rhode Island)
William Roth, Jr. (R-Delaware)
John Heinz, (R-Pennsylvania)
Malcolm Wallop, (R-Wyoming)
William Armstrong, (R-Colorado)
Steven Symms, (R-Idaho)
Charles Grassley, (R-Iowa)

Lloyd Bensten, (D-Texas)
Spark Matsunaga, (D-Hawaii)
David Boren, (D-Oklahoma)
Max Baucus, (D-Montana)
Bill Bradley, (D-New Jersey)
Daniel Moynihan, (D-New York)
George Mitchell, (D-Maine)

V.   U.S.-Israel Free Trade Area: The Negotiation Process

This chapter examines the expectations and objectives with which the United States and Israel entered into the FTA negotiations. It traces the evolution of both countries' expectations through the course of the negotiations, with particular attention to the textile and agriculture sectors. The chapter concludes by analyzing how each country fared in the negotiations and the way the final FTA agreement was reached.

A.   Initial Objectives and Opening Moves

The United States and Israel each entered the FTA negotiations with several key economic objectives.[1] Israel's primary economic objective was to maintain duty-free treatment for the GSP items. A second objective was to obtain concessions in textiles, its main industrial sector not eligible for GSP. The primary U.S. objective was the trade policy goal of negotiating a free trade area, which would further its new policy of bilateral trade liberalization. Its two

---

[1]Although there were also political objectives for both the U.S. and Israel, numerous interviews by the author of U.S. and Israeli officials confirmed that these objectives were not the major motivation for the FTA. As such the political objectives of both countries will not be addressed in this study.

main economic interests in the FTA were first to obtain
from Israel's the same tariff preferences that it gave
to the EEC (under the Israel-EEC Preference Agreement),
and second, to eliminate Israel's export subsidies and
have Israel become a signatory to the GATT Subsidies
Code.

Because of the small volume of its dutiable exports to
the U.S., Israel believed that the FTA would not be
beneficial if any product categories were excluded from
tariff elimination. It laid this out as a precondition
for negotiating the agreement.[2] The U.S. agreed to
negotiate a free trade area that would ultimately
include all the goods traded between the two countries
with no exclusions. The United States also believed
that the agreement should not have any exclusions if it
were to be considered legal under the GATT.

One of the key problems encountered throughout the FTA
negotiations was the different expectations of the two
participants. Israel was expecting a negotiation
similar to the one it concluded with the EEC fifteen
years earlier-- one of a small, less developed country

---

[2]Semadar interview, May 6, 1985.

negotiating with a large developed country.[3] The Israel-EEC Preferential Agreement recognized that Israel was the less developed party in the agreement, and allowed a fourteen year gap between the date the EEC eliminated its tariffs on exports from Israel and the date that Israel eliminates its tariffs on exports from the EEC. The United States, on the other hand, viewed the FTA as a completely reciprocal agreement between two equal parties.

Expecting a repeat of their negotiation with the EEC, Israeli officials were unprepared for the fact that the U.S. expected substantial concessions from Israel. In the early stages of the negotiations, for example, Israel wanted a ten year phase-out period for its tariffs and a four to six year phase-out period for the U.S. tariffs.[4] U.S. negotiators, however, insisted on an equal phase-out period for both countries. Most Israeli officials, unfamiliar with American trade politics, found it difficult to understand why the U.S.

---

[3]This view was repeated by a number of Israeli officials the author interviewed, including Ministry of Trade and Industry officals, Gabriela Cohen and Moshe Semadar, amd Shmuel Cohen, Assistant to the Deputy Director General for Foreign Trade, at the Ministry of Agriculture.

[4]Shmuel Cohen, Assistant to the Deputy Director General for Foreign Trade, at the Ministry of Agriculture, interview by author, Tel Aviv, May 16, 1985.

negotiated so aggressively on every tariff item when, almost across the board, Israeli imports amounted to such a negligible percentage of total U.S. imports.

While the ITC initiated its investigation on February 8, 1984 with a projected completion date of May 30, 1984, actual negotiations on the proposed FTA started on January 17, 1984. Since the United States could not start negotiating on tariffs until the ITC had issued its report, the first few months of negotiations focused on the nontariff side of the agreement, and on developing a formula for the tariff negotiations.[5]

Israeli negotiators were frustrated during the first few months of the nontariff negotiations because they felt they were making more concessions than the United States. In the area of subsidies, Israel agreed to eliminate within six years its export subsidies on industrial goods and processed agricultural products, in order to meet with the requirements of the GATT Subsidies Code. In three nontariff areas, Israel agreed to impose greater discipline than is required by the international standards set by the GATT. Israel acquiesced to eliminate the use performance requirements as a

_____

[5]Adams interview, July 31, 1985. Adams served as the chair of the interagency taskforce that coordinated U.S. positions throught the FTA negotiations.

condition for foreign investors receiving government incentives, and to restrict its right to apply protective measures to benefit its infant industries during the ten year phase-in period.[6] Israel was also willing to restrict its application of trade measures designed to alleviate balance of payments difficulties.

Israeli negotiators were most frustrated with the unwillingness of the U.S. to give them many of the nontariff concessions they had hoped for. The key non-tariff concession they had hoped for was exclusion from U.S. unfair trade provisions such as countervailing duties and antidumping duties. In addition, Israel was interested in the complete elimination of the "buy--America" provisions with regard to government procure-ment from Israel,[7] and a larger cheese quota, which the U.S. felt it could not grant for domestic political reasons.[8]

---

[6]Any duties temporarily imposed for infant industry reasons must by in place by December 31, 1990 and be removed by January 1, 1995.

[7]The agreement specifies that both countries will waive their right to "buy-national" restrictions on either countries' government purchases of goods ex-ceeding $50,000.

[8]Although the agreement permits each country to maintain nontariff import restrictions on agricultural products, Israel had wanted to negotiate the reduction of U.S. section 22 quotas, particularly on cheese.

Before the completion of the ITC report, the U.S. and
Israel also spent some of the early negotiating sessions
discussing a tariff- cutting formula for the tariff
portion of the agreement. They agreed that each side
would divide the dutiable goods on their customs list
into three categories of products: products that would
receive immediate duty-free treatment, products of
medium sensitivity which would receive duty-free
treatment in five years, and products of extreme
sensitivity which would receive duty-free treatment in
ten years. It was also agreed that each country would
follow the guideline of putting all nonsensitive items
with tariffs of less than 10% in the first category, and
all items of medium sensitivity and tariffs of more than
10% in the five year category.[9]

Both countries decided to strive for a balance in the
agreement in terms of percent of dutiable trade per
tranche. The final result was an approximate balance of
tariff concessions at the five-year mark, with the
U.S. putting more items in the immediate category and
Israel putting more items in the five-year category.[10]
The U.S. finished with 80.4% of its dutiable imports

[9]Adams interview, July 31, 1985.

[10]Ibid.

from Israel in the first tranche and 5.4% of its
dutiable imports in the second tranche, for a total of
85.8% of imports from Israel in the first two tranches.
Israel ended up with 52.5% of its dutiable imports from
the U.S. in the first tranche and 31.5% of its dutiable
imports in the second tranche, for a total of 84% of
imports from the U.S. in the first two tranches.

On the U.S. side, before the publication of the ITC
report, the Trade Policy Subcommittee (TPSC) decided
which tariff items should be considered moderately
sensitive or extremely sensitive in terms of the
negotiation. Each agency compiled a list of products
they considered import sensitive. For example, the
representative from the Department of Agriculture
compiled a list of agricultural products considered by
his agency to be sensitive, the representative from the
Department of Labor compiled a list of products
considered sensitive by his agency (perhaps industries
with a high level of unemployment or unskilled workers
that are difficult to retrain), and so on.

The lists compiled by each agency were submitted to the
TPSC and combined with items that had been identified as

sensitive by Congress or industry advisory groups.[11] In
March and April 1984, the TPSC voted on all this list of
items that were considered sensitive by any of the
agencies, industry advisory groups, or Congress. Each
item was given a vote of medium or extreme sensitivity.
Any products not voted on were placed in a tranche
according to the formulation agreed to by the two countries.[12] The initial list submitted by the U.S. was
created using the following formula:[13]

M = TPSC vote of medium sensitivity

L = TPSC vote of extreme sensitivity

Immediate duty-elimination: all items with tariffs less
than 10% and not voted M or L.

Duty elimination in five years: all items with tariffs
equal to or over 10% and not voted L and all items with
tariffs under 10% and voted M.

Duty elimination in 10 years: all items voted L.

The TPSC voted on almost all the items with imports from
Israel, items that were heavily protected with tariff or

---

[11]Various industry advisory groups provide advisory
input to the Executive branch on trade policy decisions.

[12]A very high percentage of the items with trade
were voted on by the TPSC; those items that were decided
by formula were those of absolutely no sensitivity, or
in the majority of the cases, no bilateral trade.

[13]Greg Schoephle, International Economist, Department of Labor, Interview by author, Washington D.C.,
August 15, 1985, and Adams interview, July 31, 1985.

nontariff barriers, products that had received protection as a result of an import relief, antidumping, or countervailing duty case, or products that were known to be of concern to Congress; in short, products that had been treated with care in previous negotiations. The items that were handled according to the agreed to formula were generally items with low levels of protection and no bilateral trade.

Administration officials said privately that items such as watches and clocks, glass, slide fasteners, ball bearings, dairy products, and footwear, items which, for the most part Israel does not export, but which are of traditional concern to Congress, were put in the five and ten-year categories. This was primarily for symbolic reasons-- so that the Administration could show the Congress that they were exercising care.

After the TPSC completed its report in May 1984, the TPSC added a new category of L* to denote the 43 items that were designated by ITC report as sensitive.

In Israel, the list of sensitive products was developed jointly by the Government, primarily the Ministry of Trade and Industry, and the Manufacturers' Association, an umbrella organization, representing the majority of

Israel's manufacturing sector. Each developed a list of products considered moderately sensitive to U.S. exports, and a list of products considered extremely sensitive to U.S. exports. Both used the following general criteria to assess a product's sensitivity:[14]

1) Labor variables: number of workers in each factory and in the whole sector;

2) Development areas: level of concentration of factories in development areas;

3) Production variables: percent of total consumption that is imported and/or percent of total production that is exported;

4) Main supplier to the Israeli market;

5) Level of protection: current tariff level and nontariff barriers;

6) Relative competitiveness compared to the U.S.: examination of relative prices, economies of scale, and prices of inputs in the U.S. and Israel in each sector;

7) Level of development: sophistication of sector, and potential for growth and development.

Although MTI and MA each compiled a list of products

[14]Moshe Nahum, Director of International Trade, Manufacturer's Association, of Israel, interview by author, Tel Aviv, March 20, 1985, and Gabriela Cohen, International Economist, Ministry of Trade and Industry, interview by author, Jerusalem, May 15, 1985.

considered sensitive, these lists were very informal.
The Ministry of the Treasury also identified items
considered sensitive in terms of revenue generation. It
was not until mid-August, however, that MTI and MA
crafted a joint list of products considered moderately
and extremely sensitive to U.S. imports. This list
became Israel's initial offer.[15]

B. The Negotiation Process and Subsequent Moves

After being frustrated with the nontariff negotiations,
the Israeli negotiators were even more frustrated when
both countries began exchanging tariff offers. In early
August 1984, the United States surprised Israel by
informally presenting Israeli negotiators with an offer
list of items for immediate, five-year and ten-year
tariff elimination, as well as a list of tariff concessions they wanted from Israel.[16] Israel was surprised by the comprehensiveness of the U.S. list-- all
Israel had put together by August was a "negative
request list," items that it was willing to see the
U.S. put in its five or ten-year tariff-elimination
category. After seeing the type of list that the
U.S. presented, Israeli negotiators went back to the

---

[15]Nahum interview, March 20, 1985.

[16]S. Cohen interview, May 16, 1985.

drawing board and put together an offer list of items for immediate, five-year, and ten-year tariff elimination in a very short period of time.[17]

On August 31, both countries formally exchanged their initial offers. Israel's initial offer had a much higher percentage of its tariff items in the first and second tranches than did the initial U.S. offer,[18] which was more "padded," leaving room for negotiation. After seeing the U.S. initial offer, Israel maintained that it could not conclude an agreement unless the U.S. made substantial changes in its tariff-offer package. When this imbalance in initial offers occurred, the U.S. realized that it had to offer more on the tariff portion of the negotiation since it was unwilling to offer Israel more of what it wanted in the nontariff portion of the negotiation. As a result, the U.S. made almost all of the tariff concessions during the remaining negotiation sessions.

After the initial tariff offers, the U.S. made four subsequent offers in the nontextile negotiations, and four offers dealing only with textile products, while Israel made only two subsequent offers before an

---

[17]G. Cohen interview, May 15, 1985.

[18]Adams interview July 31, 1985.

agreement could be achieved.[19]   Between the initial and final U.S. nontextile offers, the U.S. made continued concessions, moving tariff items forward, from the third tranche to the second, and from the second to the first. Israel, overall, pulled back concessions it had initially offered, once it saw the U.S. opening offer and realized that it had offered more than the United States.

In addition to Israel's misconception that the U.S. would treat it as a less developed country rather than as an equal trading partner, it misunderstood the politics of U.S. trade policy and the domestic pressures under which the U.S. negotiators were operating. Israel assumed that since, from a purely economic perspective, none of their imports threatened any U.S. sector, the U.S. would have no trouble making concessions in the negotiations. Israel did not take into account the political pressure from the Congress and its constituency with which U.S. negotiators had to contend.

Congressional pressure on the negotiation escalated at the third negotiation session on November 6, when the

---

[19]The U.S. made subsequent nontextile tariff offers on September 5, 1984, November 6, 1984, November 9, 1984, and January 15, 1985. Israel made two subsequent offers on November 5, 1984 and January 15, 1985.

United States informed Israel of its decision that the
items identified as sensitive by the ITC would have
their tariffs frozen for ten years, and that this
decision was not negotiable. In the first two negotiation sessions (August 31 and September 5), U.S.
negotiators had put the items identified by the ITC in a
separate tranche, although agreement between the
Administration and the Congress on how to handle these
items was not reached until late September. Up until
its final offer on January 15, Israel still had all its
items in three categories, immediate, five year, and ten
year. In response to the U.S. declaration of its frozen
list, Israel presented the U.S. at the final negotiation session with its own, much longer list of items
on which tariffs would be frozen. Israel also asserted
its frozen list was not negotiable. Thus, no negotiation took place on either of the frozen lists. Both
lists remained unchanged and appear in their original
form in the final agreement.[20]

Tables 1 through 4 illustrate a notable feature of the
negotiations. They reveal that the U.S. did remarkably
little shifting between categories during the negotiations. To a large extent, this illustrates the
strict political constraints within which the

---

[20]Wignot interview, January 14, 1985.

U.S. negotiators had to operate, resulting in their limited ability to make concessions. Out of a total of 10,349 dutiable U.S. tariff items, only 396 tariff items were moved forward to tranches with faster tariff elimination between the initial and final U.S. offers. Between Israel's initial and final offers, 366 items shifted categories, almost all moving backward from the third tranche to the newly created fourth tranche in the final negotiation session.

Agriculture

Of the nontextile negotiations, agriculture posed the greatest difficulty. The initial position of the U.S. Department of Agriculture (USDA) was that it wanted to totally exclude all agriculture products from the FTA agreement.[21] Because the key U.S. agriculture exports to Israel (primarily grains) are duty free, USDA believed that it had no export interest in keeping agriculture in the agreement.[22] As a result, its key aim was to protect U.S. farmers from Israeli imports. Once it became clear that USTR Brock was not going to budge from his position of including all sectors in the

---

[21]Article 6 of the FTA allows the maintaining of administrative import restrictions on agricultural products, so that in many cases the removal of tariffs still left significant import restrictions.

[22]Adams interview, July 31, 1985.

negotiations, USDA focused its efforts on eliminating Israel's agricultural subsidies and excluding the items identified by the ITC, a majority of which were agricultural products.

In the August meetings, the United States, at the behest of Congress and the USDA, demanded that Israel eliminate its agricultural subsidies. Israel maintained that it would eliminate the subsidies required by the Subsidies Code, but no more.[23] Israel refused to move on this issue stating that 90% of its agricultural exports go to the EEC market, and that it needed its subsidies in order to compete against the subsidized EEC agricultural products. It also became clear to the U.S. negotiators that the U.S. could not ask Israel to eliminate its agricultural subsidies while the U.S. retained its own agricultural subsidies.[24] USDA was particularly concerned about this issue because most of Israel's subsidies are for fruits and vegetables, Israel's major agricultural exports to the United States. In the U.S., on the other hand, fruits and vegetables are not protected by production subsidies like many other U.S. agricultural sectors.

---

[23]S. Cohen interview, May 16, 1985.

[24]Adams interview, July 31, 1985.

Having lost these two fights, USDA realized that
agriculture would be included in the agreement, but
still did not support the FTA. As a result, USDA
negotiators took a passive approach during the remainder
of the negotiations and did not participate in a number
of the negotiation sessions, leaving USTR to make the
decisions as to which concessions to make in
agriculture.[25]

The Case of Textiles

The textile portion of the FTA negotiation was by far
the most difficult to negotiate for several reasons.
The textile sector is the most heavily protected
industrial sector in the U.S. with a well-organized
industry and strong political support. On the Israeli
side, textiles were of particular interest as the key
sector with extensive tariff and nontariff barriers
which did not receive duty-free treatment under GSP. In
return for opening its market to the United States,
Israel believed it should receive something more than it
was receiving under GSP. This meant that it had to
receive concessions from the U.S. in the two key areas
not covered by GSP-- agriculture and textiles. Due to
distance, transportation costs, and perishability, fresh
agriculture from Israel does not offer a large export

---

[25]Ibid.

opportunity. Textiles, therefore, remained the critical
area. Under GSP and MFN, 93.1% of Israel's goods
already entered the United States duty-free in 1983.
Twenty percent of the remaining dutiable trade was in
textiles and apparel.[26]

Israel's negotiators felt that Israel would have to
receive substantial textile concessions from the United
States in order to sign the agreement.[27] In addition,
Israel's textile industry, believing that it could
potentially be the main beneficiary from a free trade
area with the United States, was vigorously opposed to
any agreement that did not offer it immediate
benefits.[28] This is particularly true because textile
and apparel imports into the U.S. have among the highest
tariffs of any U.S. sector, averaging 20-30%.

The entire negotiation on textiles consisted of the U.S.
making offers and Israel claiming it needed more
concessions for the agreement to be worthwhile from its
perspective. The U.S. made a total of four separate

---

[26]U.S. Department of Commerce, Import Monthly,
series 145, Washington D.C. 1983.

[27]Semadar interview, May 6, 1985.

[28]Yoram Radoshitzky, Chairman of the Textile Board,
Manufacturer's Association of Israel, interview by
author, Tel Aviv, May 23, 1985.

offers on textiles: on November 9, 1984; November 20, 1984; January 11, 1985; and January 23, 1985. U.S. negotiators knew that they could not exclude a sector from the agreement, particularly not a sector that had not been identified by the ITC. Yet they recognized the extreme political sensitivity of the textile issue.[29] The initial U.S. tariff offer to Israel on August 31, placed almost all the textile and apparel items in the category with tariff elimination in ten years (there was not yet a freeze category at this time). Israel responded to this offer by saying that it could not sign an agreement without some textile and apparel items in the first two categories.[30] Minister Patt told USTR Brock that Israel needed some "big ticket" textile items in the first category in order to be able to sign the agreement.[31] At this point, the U.S. moved ladies swimsuits, the largest single textile item (in terms of Israel's exports to the U.S.), into the immediate tariff elimination category. After this U.S. offer, however, the Israeli textile industry told its government that this concession was not adequate since this only

---

[29]Don Eiss, Senior Policy Analyst, Department of Commerce, interview by author, Washington D.C., July 25, 1985.

[30]Radoshitzky interview, May 23, 1985.

[31]Adams interview, July 31, 1985.

benefited one small segment of the industry.[32] Israel then presented the U.S. with a list of textile items for which it wanted immediate tariff elimination. In response, the U.S. side began searching for other textile tariff items that could be moved into the immediate or five year tariff elimination categories. Although they moved a few textile tariff items where there was no trade, it became apparent that, because of political pressure, almost no five-digit tariff items existed that could be moved out of the ten-year category. It was at this point, at the November 11 negotiating session, that the U.S. negotiators decided to take the unusual step of moving to a seven-digit tariff negotiation on textiles so that they would be able to move more items out of the ten-year category.[33] Israel responded with another request, and the U.S. made another offer on November 20. At this time, the U.S. decided to change the tariff elimination schedule for the ten-year category so that the tariff reductions would be skewed towards the first five years, with 60% tariff elimination at the five-year mark. Israel accepted these concessions, and the textile negotiation impasse was broken.

---

[32]Radoshitzky interview, May 23, 1985.

[33]Adams interview, July 31, 1985. The seven-digit tariff categories are more disaggregated than the five-digit tariff categories.

On March 31, 1985, shortly after the FTA had been initialed, the Department of Commerce issued a call on cotton flannel sheets from Israel.[34] The Committee on the Implementation of Textile Agreements (CITA) set the level for Israeli imports of flannel sheets at 600,000 units.[35] The Israeli government responded immediately, stating that the call violated the FTA agreement and threatening not to implement the FTA. The United States claimed it had clearly stated that the FTA agreement did not supercede other U.S. statutes, including the MFA.[36]

---

[34]Israel does not have a bilateral textile agreement with the U.S. that sets specific quota limits on all textile items exported to the U.S. Imports from all countries without bilateral textile agreements are monitored by the Committee for the Implementation of Textile Agreements (CITA) in the Commerce Department. CITA monitors imports not covered by bilateral agreements and issues a "call" if there is "market disruption" or threat thereof by imports. A call is a request for consultations with the specific purpose of setting an import limit for the product involved. In deciding whether there is market disruption, CITA considers the overall growth in imports from a particular supplier, the ratio of imports to domestic production, and a host of other factors. These criteria, however, are only guidelines; the decision itself is discretionary. Both the industry and the Congress can request CITA to examine the import figures for a particular product.

[35]Eve Anderson, Industry Analyst, Office of International Textile Agreements, Department of Commerce, telephone interview by author, Washington D.C., August 6, 1985.

[36]Section 5 of the implementing legislation specifies that "No provision of the Agreement nor the application of any such provision... which is in conflict with ... any statute of the United States shall be given effect under the laws of the United States."

This disagreement continued throughout the summer months and threatened to destroy implementation of the whole FTA agreement, the tariff portion of which was scheduled to enter into force on September 1, 1985.

After a number of consultations and high-level pressure, Israel agreed to sign the FTA, and to negotiate a separate bilateral quota for Israeli textile imports into the United States. The Israeli Cabinet implemented the FTA on August 18, 1985. The negotiations toward a bilateral textile agreement proceeded slowly for several months. On October 8, 1985 CITA put a hold on flannel sheet imports from Israel, claiming that the initial quota of 600,00 units was almost filled, and a new import limit of 750,000 units was negotiated.[37] Although negotiations proceeded on a bilateral textile agreement, the two sides were still not able to reach a final agreement. On February 24, 1986 CITA put an embargo on Israeli flannel sheet imports, claiming that the new limit had been exceeded.[38] At this announcement the Israeli government balked at signing the bilateral quota agreement. After two weeks of intensive nego-

---

[37]Ron Sorini, International Economist, Office of Textile Negotiations, Office of the U.S. Trade Representative, interview by author, Washington D.C., April 2, 1986.

[38]Ibid.

tiations, it became clear that the differences sur-
rounding the bilateral agreement could not be resolved.
Negotiations on the bilateral textile agreement broke
down on March 12, 1986, with both sides agreeing to
abandon the attempt to negotiate such an agreement.[39]

C. Summary

The U.S. negotiators had the difficult job of trying to
negotiate an agreement that would address the concerns
of Congress and still be acceptable to Israel as well.
Because the TPSC members knew that any agreement would
eventually have to be passed by Congress, they tried to
craft the initial U.S. offer in such a way as to
anticipate Congressional concerns. Most of these
concerns were well known to the Administration since
they involved industries that had been the subject of
special treatment in other trade negotiations or in
tariff liberalizing legislation. In examining how the
initial U.S. offer was crafted, it is clear that
avoiding politically sensitive items and anticipating
Congressional concerns were more important goals than
identifying industries that could potentially suffer

---

[39]Ibid. Since the U.S. and Israel did not reach a
bilateral agreement on textiles, Israel's textile
imports to the U.S. are still monitored by CITA and
subject to calls at any time.

legitimate labor adjustment difficulties as a result of
duty elimination to Israel. This is evident in the fact
that items with tariffs over 10% were automatically
placed in the later tariff elimination tranches in the
initial U.S. offer. In doing this, the negotiators were
ensuring that the existing tariff structure would be
maintained in the FTA.

Concern with maintaining the historical structure of
protection can also be seen in the case of the textile
industry. The textile case illustrates the power of the
textile lobby in the U.S. Its strength is such that the
issue was dealt with out of the context of the main
negotiations. This special treatment was accorded
despite the fact that the tariff negotiations were
relatively insignificant in comparison to the industry's
quota protection under the MFA, and the fact that the
ITC did not even cite the textile industry as being
sensitive to imports from Israel. It is nonetheless
important to point out that U.S. negotiators achieved a
policy victory by succeeding in including the textile
sector in the agreement and eventually eliminating
tariffs on that sector, given the pressure from Congress
to exclude the textile sector from the FTA, as it was
from CBI and GSP.

This chapter analyzed the negotiation process and showed the drive to maintain the existing structure of protection within the context of the FTA. Chapter VI is an empirical analysis of the outcome of the negotiations which will seek to confirm what has been demonstrated in this chapter.

NEGOTIATION OFFERS BY THE U.S. AND ISRAEL

Table 1

Initial U.S. Offer

All Items

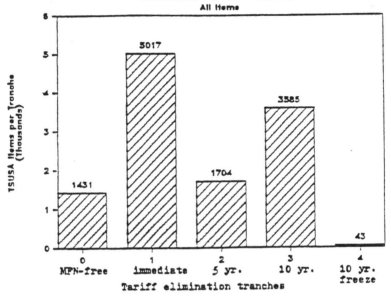

Table 2

Final U.S. Offer

All Items

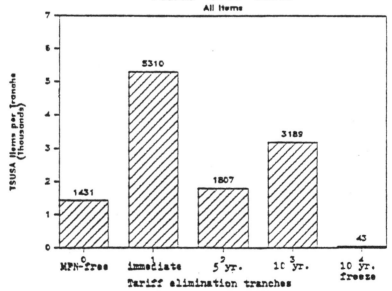

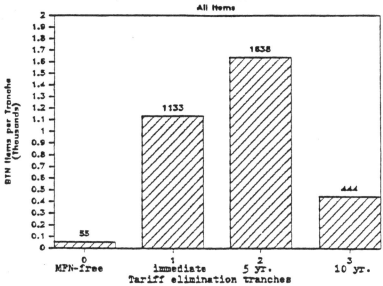

Table 3
Initial Israeli Offer
All Items

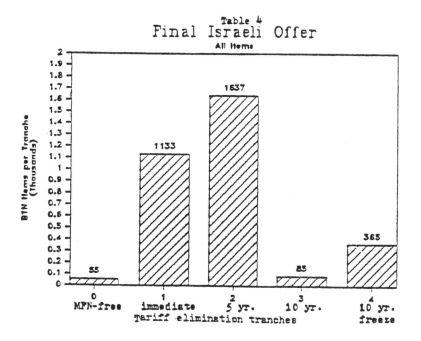

Table 4
Final Israeli Offer
All Items

VI. Empirical Analysis

This chapter sets out to formally test the hypothesis
that the level of protection an item had before the FTA
provides the best indicator of how the item was dealt
with in the FTA negotiations. We do this by constructing a statistical model that tests this hypothesis. The first section of the chapter discusses the
hypothesis and presents a statistical model constructed
to test it, while the second section explains the
variables used in the model and their expected signs.
The chapter concludes with a discussion of the empirical
results.

A. The Model and the Hypothesis

In the model constructed to predict the tranche into
which an item was placed during the negotiations, the
dependent variable, the tranche, is characterized by the
fact that it is ordered and discrete. One way to model
such a variable is to use multichotomous probit analysis. This type of analysis provides a framework for
modeling problems where observations fall into X
mutually exclusive groups, and the groups are assumed to

be ordered from 1 to X.[1] In the present case, we are working with tariff items that will fall into one of four tranches, ordered from one to four. The multichotomous probit model is used to estimate situations where z_i is equal to 0 if the observations of z_i^* are in one category, or z_i is equal to 1 if the observations of z_i^* are in a second category, or z_i is equal to 2 if the observations of z_i^* are in a third category, and so on. Generalizing the case of the simple probit model, the multichotomous probit model allows us to compute z_i from the cumulative normal probability function, for each actual observation z_i^*. The multichotomous probit model assumes that there are cutoff points z^* and z^{**} which define the relationship between the observed and unobserved dependent variables. Specifically, in the case of a single explanatory variable, $z_i = a + bx_i$ and,

$$z_i = 2 \quad \text{if} \quad z_i^* \geq z^{**}$$
$$z_i = 1 \quad \text{if} \quad z^* < z_i^* < z^{**}$$
$$z_i = 0 \quad \text{if} \quad z_i^* \leq z^*$$

---

[1]The reader who is interested in the derivation of the multichotomous probit model is refered to Maddala, G.S., <u>Limited Dependent and Qualitative Variables in Econometrics</u>, (Cambridge: Cambridge University Press, 1983), and Pindyck, Robert S., and Daniel L. Rubinfeld, <u>Econometric Models and Economic Forecasting</u>, (New York: McGraw-Hill Book Company, 1981), chapter 2.

The parameters of the model are estimated using a maximum likelihood nonlinear estimation routine, which estimates the probability of the dependent variable falling into a particular group. Here this technique is used to estimate the probability of an individual item falling into a particular tranche.

In constructing our model, we refer to the studies reviewed in chapter II describing the characteristics of industries that successfully obtained protection. Many of these studies demonstrated that industries with high tariffs were not only the most successful at obtaining protection but received the lowest duty cuts in tariff liberalizing negotiations. Furthermore, industries with high tariffs generally had powerful political backing in Congress, and were thus successful in maintaining that protection. This chapter uses the level of protection (tariff and nontariff barriers) prior to the FTA negotiation as an indication of how negotiators would treat individual products during the course of the FTA negotiations. As documented in the previous chapter, U.S. negotiators indicated that existing tariff levels were used in crafting the initial U.S. offer to Israel. This, in fact, is a tacit acknowledgement by U.S. negotiators of tariff rates as a proxy for political sensitivity.

Testing whether our variables have the hypothesized effect will accomplish three goals. First, it will formally confirm our anecdotal information that U.S. negotiators used the existing level of protection as the key criterion in crafting their initial offer to Israel. Second, it will show that nontariff barriers, as well as tariff rates, were used to determine an item's tranche placement. Finally, it will show that these criteria were not only used to craft the initial offer, but more importantly, were maintained throughout the negotiations, and into the final agreement.

This study postulates that negotiators use the level of protection itself, as opposed to information on import sensitivity, as a guide for determining a product's treatment in a liberalizing negotiation. Data on labor adjustment costs are available on an industry-wide basis, according to the Standard Industry Classification (SIC), while trade negotiations are conducted on a product basis, following the Tariff Schedule of the United States of America (TSUSA). There are 371 SIC categories in contrast to over 10,000 five-digit TSUSA categories. Since negotiations are conducted on a highly disaggregated level, the level of protection is the product-specific information that negotiators have

available and can use as a proxy for a product's sensitivity. Since an item's tariff level typically
reflects the political motivations for protection at
least as strongly as the economic motivations, the
result is that items with political sensitivities are
protected in trade negotiations.

The model developed in this chapter will test the hypothesis that the shape of the agreement was determined by
the existing levels of protection on a product-by
product basis; this hypothesis will be tested against
the results of the actual agreement. The model attempts
to predict the tranches in which items were placed in
the negotiations, based on their level of protection
prior to the FTA negotiation. The availability of a
sample with over 10,000 items provides a particularly
good opportunity to test the model and determine the
degree of its predictive power.

The data used in this analysis document the tariff
offers made by the U.S. and Israel, across the entire
tariff schedule, from the initiation of the FTA negotiations to the completion of an agreement.[2]

---

[2]The offers from the textile and nontextile negotiations were merged in order to obtain an across-the-
board documentation of U.S. offers.

B. The Variables and their Expected Signs

Working from the hypothesis that negotiators use the existing level of protection to determine an item's tranche placement in the agreement, we start by using tariff rates as the first variable reflecting an item's level of protection. A variable representing each item's 1984 ad valorem tariff rate is used in the model. It is expected to have a positive sign because we suspect that U.S. negotiators agreed to eliminate tariffs immediately on products with low tariffs. Conversely, we suspect that the products which negotiators perceived as politically sensitive, and thus placed in later tranches, were those with higher tariffs.[3]

Similarly, we suspect that negotiators would put items eligible for duty-free treatment under the GSP program in the tranche for immediate duty elimination, and items not eligible for GSP treatment in tranches for later tariff elimination. Lack of GSP eligibility is significant not only because it effects an item's tariff level but also because it indicates a certain degree of political sensitivity in an industry. First, a number of politically sensitive industries, such as textiles,

---

[3]See Appendix I to this chapter for a complete definition of each variable in the model.

are specifically excluded from the GSP program by
legislation. Second, industries can petition to be
excluded from the GSP program if import levels in a
given product reach certain levels.[4] For this second
variable, a dummy variable is used to indicate whether
or not a product is eligible for duty-free treatment
under the GSP program. This variable is expected to
have a positive sign, meaning that items eligible for
GSP are in earlier tranches and items not eligible are
in the later tranches.

The third variable indicates whether an item is protected by nontariff barriers, and in particular,
product-specific quotas. Items under quota include
textile items under the Multifiber Arrangement, dairy
products under the Department of Agriculture's Section
22 quotas, and items under quota as a result of an
escape clause case. It was expected that all items
under quota are politically sensitive and hence that
negotiators would put items with quotas in tranches
after those items without quotas. Two dummy variables,
one to indicate the presence of textile quotas and
another one to indicate the presence of nontextile
quotas were used in the model. Both variables are

---

[4]See chapter III for a complete discussion of the
GSP program's eligibility rules.

expected to have a positive sign.

The last variable used in this model is a measure of whether a particular item is exported by Israel to the United States.   It was suspected that items exported from Israel to the U.S. would be regarded by U.S. nego-tiators as more import sensitive, and items without imports from Israel would be considered less import sensitive.   As such, we expect that a dummy variable indicating the presence of imports from Israel will have a positive sign, that is, the presence of trade would lead negotiators to place items in a tranche for delayed tariff elimination.

Appendix I to this chapter has a complete description of the data used in this chapter as well a description of each variable.

C. Empirical Results

The model was run against the final U.S. offer, first using only tariffs as an explanatory variable (equation 1, Table 1), and subsequently with tariffs and textile quotas as explanatory variables (equation 2, Table 1). As we see in Table 2, tariffs alone had almost a 65% accuracy rate in predicting the tranches into which

items would be placed in the final offer. Tariffs and
textile quotas taken together had an 80.2% accuracy
rate; this was very close to the 80.4% accuracy rate
obtained using the entire model with all five explanatory variables to predict the final offer (equation 3,
Table 1). In equation 3 the model predicted correctly
into which tranches 8,321 out of 10,349 tariff items
were placed in the final offer. Using all five variables to predict the initial offer resulted in an 82.6%
accuracy rate (equation 4, Table 1). In equation 4 the
model had a very high level of predictive power, placing
8,548 out of 10,349 items in the correct tranches.

As hypothesized, the level of protection prior to the
negotiation was the key determinant in how items were
treated in the course of the negotiation. Tariff rates
(AVE84) were the most significant explanatory variable
in determining the placement of items in tranches.
Interestingly, the nominal tariff rate was much more
statistically significant in determining how a product
would be staged, as opposed to whether or not the
product was already entering the U.S. duty free under
the GSP program (GSP). There were items with high tariff
rates that were put in the second, third, and fourth
tranches that were actually entering, and would

TABLE 1

EMPIRICAL RESULTS

Equation	VARIABLES				
	AVE84 Coefficients	TEX	QUO	GSP	TRAD
1	0.0718* (51.88)				
2	0.0414* (25.45)	2.4037* (69.01)			
3	0.0409* (24.84)	2.3982* (67.32)	0.5668* (5.31)	0.0469 (0.59)	−0.3039* (−5.17)
4	0.0612* (34.21)	2.5182* (68.59)	0.5464* (5.09)	0.3755* (4.90)	0.1419* (2.37)

Equation 1 -- final offer with AVE84 only.
Equation 2 -- final offer with AVE84 and TEX only.
Equation 3 -- final offer with all five explanatory variables.
Equation 4 -- initial offer with all five explanatory variables.

The numbers in parentheses below the coefficients are the t-statistics. The star (*) indicates that the variable is significant at the 95% significance level.

TABLE 2

ACCURACY OF MODEL's PREDICTED RESULTS

Equation	Percent Accurately Predicted				
	Overall	Tranche			
		1	2	3	4
1	64.9	94.6	40.0	30.6	0
2	80.2	95.7	3.3	99.2	0
3	80.4	95.8	4.5	99.2	0
4	82.6	96.2	13.0	97.8	0

Equation 1 -- final offer with AVE84 only.
Equation 2 -- final offer with AVE84 and TEX only.
Equation 3 -- final offer with all five explanatory
variables.
Equation 4 -- initial offer with all five explanatory
variables.

continue to enter, the U.S. on a duty-free basis under the GSP program.[5] Although GSP was significant in the initial offer, it was not significant in the final offer. Thus, while a product's eligibility for GSP was a factor in crafting the initial offer, it was less important during the negotiations when nominal tariff rates became an overriding factor.

Whether or not an item was under quota was statistically significant in determining the tranche into which that item was placed. While textile (TEX) and nontextile quotas (QUO) were significant in the model, TEX was a much more powerful predictor than QUO. Clearly the negotiators felt that textile items, which are heavily protected, should be placed in the later tranches, even though Israel exports very few textile items to the U.S. Ninety percent of the textile items were placed in the third tranche in the initial offer. By the final offer, that number had gone down slightly but was still an overwhelming 82%. Of the 130 nontextile TSUSA items that were under quota at the time of the FTA negotiations, 86 were dairy products under Section 22 agricultural quotas. Thus, in large part, the variable QUO measured the extent to which that industry was protected

---

[5]According to the FTA, eligibility under GSP would not affected during the period that tariffs are phased out.

in the negotiations. Of the 86 dairy items, Israel only exported 4 items to the U.S.

While the existence of imports from Israel (TRAD) was statistically significant in both the initial and final offers, the sign of the coefficient changed. When the model was run against the initial offer, TRAD had a negative sign. Clearly U.S. negotiators felt that items with imports from Israel should be placed in the later tranches.[6] During the course of the negotiations, however, most of the concessions demanded by Israel's negotiators were on items that it exported to the United States. As a result, by the final offer most of the items with imports from Israel had been moved to earlier tranches, and TRAD had a positive sign. Earlier equations were run using a continuous explanatory variable which measured the value of imports from Israel, however, this variable was not significant in any of the equations.

Looking at Table 2, we see that the model was a much better predictor of the items falling into tranche 1 or

---

[6]Although the majority of Israel's exports to the U.S. entered duty-free under MFN or GSP, the items that entered under MFN were not part of the negotiation. TRAD includes all the items with imports from Israel that were dutiable at the time of the negotiaiton, including those that were enjoying temporary duty-free treatment under the GSP program.

tranche 3 than of those falling into tranche 2. U.S. negotiators placed most of the items that had relatively low protection before the FTA in tranche 1, and those with relatively high protection in tranche 3. The model was quite accurate in predicting these items at either extreme of protection, however it was less accurate in predicting the items that had medium levels of protection. The model nonetheless had a high overall level of predictive ability, because the second tranche has 1,807 items in the final agreement, far fewer items than the 5,310 items in the first tranche, or the 3,189 items in the third tranche.

Despite its high predictive ability, the model seemed unable to predict the items in tranche 4, the items on the ITC list. Looking at the ITC list[7] we see that none of the items are under quota, some have high tariffs and some do not, only half of the items have imports from Israel, and some of these are eligible for GSP. It seems clear that these forty-three items were not placed into tranche 4 according to the same criteria as the other 10,306 items. In large part, these items were evaluated as extremely sensitive by the ITC because of pressure groups lobbying for their exclusion from the

---

[7]See chapter IV for a detailed discussion of the items identified by the ITC in its report.

FTA. One can conclude that negotiators use an item's existing level of protection as a guide in a negotiation, except for items where an unusual amount of political pressure is present for special treatment. Because the ITC list comprises only .4% of the total number of TSUSA items and because of the political reasons for their separate treatment, the inability to predict these items does not detract from the overall success of the model.

Clearly there may be valid economic criteria, like labor adjustment costs, to justify continuing to protect certain industries. In the case of the FTA, however, decisions about which industries to protect were based predominantly on political, rather than economic criteria. Given that the majority of Israel's imports into the U.S. entered duty-free under MFN or GSP at the time of the negotiations, the possibility of labor adjustment costs resulting from eliminating tariffs on the remaining items was negligible. The items that were not duty free at the onset of the negotiations were the ones that were placed in later tranches, the majority of which had no imports from Israel. In fact, of the 10,349 tariff items that were not MFN-free at the time of the negotiations, only 1,459 items had imports from Israel, yet 5,039 items are in tranches other than

immediate tariff elimination. Out of 3,845 textile
tariff items in the negotiation, only 223 items had any
imports from Israel, yet over 80% of textile items were
placed in the third tranche in the final agreement. The
lack of tariff concessions for both the textile items
and the other items under quota is even more remarkable,
given that tariff elimination in these product areas
would not have had a substantial effect on trade,
precisely because these items are already protected by
nontariff means which are not affected by the FTA.

The differences between the initial and the final offers
reflect the fact that the initial offer represents the
motivations and priorities of the U.S. government, while
the final offer also incorporates the give and take of
the negotiations. Nonetheless, the model still is a
very powerful predictor of the final offer. It was
noted in the previous chapter that the difference
between the initial offer and the final offer is quite
small. This observation reinforces the strength of this
study's hypothesis; the criterion used in developing the
initial offer, continuing to protect items already
protected, was so strong that the U.S. was not willing
to give significant concessions on its original offer.

APPENDIX I

Description of the Data

This analysis is based on a documentation of the tariff
offers made by the United States and Israel during
course of the U.S.-Israel FTA negotiations. The offers
comprise each country's complete tariff schedule of
goods, including those with no trade between Israel and
the United States. The data are in two files, the
documentation of the U.S. offers,[8] and the documentation
of Israel's offers. The U.S. file lists items by TSUSA
(Tariff Schedule of the United States of America)
numbers, while the Israel file lists items by BTN
(Brussels Tariff Nomenclature) numbers.

The final agreement has five tranches of goods:

    TRANCHE0-Tariff items already tariff-free on an MFN
    basis
    TRANCHE1-Tariff items with elimination of duties
    immediately upon the agreement's entry into force.
    TRANCHE2-Tariff items with elimination of duties in
    three stages by January 1, 1989.
    TRANCHE3-Tariff items with elimination of duties in
    eight stages by January 1, 1995.
    TRANCHE4-Tariff items with duties frozen for five
    years. After five years, the President will seek
    the advice of the ITC as to the timetable of tariff
    elimination on the U.S. products; however, both

---

[8]The U.S. offers were actually made in two groups,
the textile offers and the nontextile offers. These two
groups of offers were combined to obtain a combined
U.S. offer, accross the entire tariff schedule.

countries have agreed to eliminate tariffs on these products by January 1, 1995.

Both countries made their initial offers (based on the formulas discussed in chapter V) on August 31, 1984. The U.S. made four subsequent offers in the nontextile negotiations, (September 5, 1984, November 6, 1984, November 9, 1984, and January 15, 1985). Israel made two subsequent offers on November 5, 1984 and January 15, 1985. For each date, the data lists in which tranche each tariff item, not already duty-free under MFN, would be placed. This allows the evolution of the final agreement to be examined.

Description of Variables

The empirical analysis discussed in the chapter used only the U.S. offers. The variables used in the model are defined as follows:

1) Dependent variable:
The first dependent variable used was "NEG1" which was defined as the tranche placement in the initial U.S. offer. The TSUSA items that were already MFN-free at the onset of the negotiations were eliminated as these items were automatically placed in TRANCHE0. Dutiable TSUSA items that were placed in the immediate tariff elimination category (TRANCHE1) were given a value of NEG1=0. Items in TRANCHE2 were given a value of NEG1=1. Items in TRANCHE3 were given a value of NEG1=2, and items in TRANCHE4 were given a value of NEG1=3. The second dependent variable used was "NEG5" which was defined as the tranche placement in the final U.S. offer. Like NEG1, NEG5 was given values of 0,1,2 & 3, determined in the same way.

2) Independent Variables:
    a)"AVE84" - a continuous variable, defined as an

item's ad valorem tariffs in 1984

   b)"GSP" - defined as whether or not the item was
duty-free under the GSP program. GSP is a dummy
variable with a value of GSP=0 if the item is GSPfree
and GSP=1 if it is not.

   c)"TRAD" - defined as whether or not there were any
imports from Israel in that TSUSA item in 1983. TRAD is
a dummy variable with a value of TRAD=1 if there were
imports and TRAD=0 if there were none.

   d)"QUO" - defined as whether or not the TSUSA item
was under any U.S. quota arrangement at the time of the
FTA negotiations. QUO is a dummy variable with a value
of QUO=1 if there was a quota and QUO=0 for items not
under quota.

   e)"TEX" - defined as whether or not the TSUSA item
was under the Multifiber Arrangement at the time of the
FTA negotiations. TEX is a dummy variable with a value
of TEX=1 if under the Multifiber Arrangement and TEX=0
for all other items.

VII. Summary and Conclusions

This study has analyzed the political economy involved
in the negotiation of the U.S.-Israel FTA, and illustrated that the process by which the U.S. negotiates
trade agreements encourages the maintenance of the
existing structure of protection. Although all U.S.
tariffs to Israel will be eliminated over a period of
ten years, the items on which tariff elimination was
delayed fell according to predictable lines. The
preceding chapter demonstrated that the level of protection an item had before the FTA was the best
indicator of the item's treatment in the FTA negotiations. This held true even though only 0.5% of total
U.S. imports came from Israel at the time the FTA was
negotiated, and over 90% of these imports from Israel
already entered the U.S. duty free. Moreover, the FTA
maintained many nontariff barriers, some of which are
more significant barriers to trade than the tariffs. In
fact, because of the presence of these nontariff
barriers, and quotas in particular, the FTA is not
really a free trade area in the strictest economic
sense.

Understanding the political dynamics that accompanied

the negotiation of the FTA sheds light on the process by
which the U.S. negotiates all trade agreements. The
interactions among pressure groups, the Congress, and
the Executive branch that were present in the negotiation of the FTA are present in the negotiation of any
trade agreement, bilateral or multilateral. Furthermore, these same motivations and pressures play a role
in most trade policy decisions that involve the
Congress, such as the renewal of the GSP program or the
Multifiber Arrangement.

This study examined the factors in the U.S. trade policy
process that favor the continued protection of those
industries which are already heavily protected.
Although the key factors, such as constituent pressure
on Congressmen, and the consequent Congressional
pressure on the Executive branch are present throughout
the trade policy process, the negotiation of a trade
agreement is unique in certain ways. While the President has authority to implement most trade policy
decisions, he does not have the authority to implement a
trade agreement. As such, the President is mandated to
go forth and negotiate an agreement with a foreign
government or governments, and then bring this agreement
back to Congress to enact into domestic law. Because of
this constitutionally enforced partnership, the Exe-

cutive branch must have the counsel and cooperation of the Congress throughout the negotiation process in order to avoid a situation in which the Executive branch negotiates an agreement that is not implemented by the Congress. Since Congress is more subject to protectionist pressures from constituents, the pressures to maintain the existing structure of protection are stronger in the negotiation of a trade agreement, than in other trade policy decisions.

The U.S.-Israel FTA is significant because it creates a precedent for subsequent free trade areas and the Administration has announced that it favors negotiating free trade areas with other interested countries.[1] The FTA between the U.S. and Israel, however, does not necessarily represent the format for future free trade areas. For instance, while the agreement recently negotiated between the U.S. and Canada had similarities with the U.S.-Israel FTA, it differed because of the tremendous volume of trade between these two countries, their status as each other's primary trade partners, and the bilateral trade surplus the U.S. has with Canada.

Although the United States was successful in concluding

---

[1]President Ronald Reagan, speech at the Bonn Economic Summit, May 1985. The Administration signed a free trade area with Canada on January 2, 1988.

a free trade area with Canada, the group of countries with which the U.S. would attempt to negotiate a free trade area will likely remain very small. Few countries are candidates because of the strong political opposition that is involved in negotiating any free trade area. Since the pressure to maintain the existing structure of protection was so strong in an agreement where the potential economic impact resulting from imports into the U.S. was minimal, the opposition to an FTA with most other countries would undoubtedly be much greater.

Because of Israel's small size, the political dynamics of U.S.-Israel FTA were not completely representative of other U.S. trade negotiations. Negotiations involving larger countries elicit interest from industry groups, and consequently Congressmen, that want increased access to the foreign market(s). With some isolated exceptions, almost no pressure on behalf of U.S. industry was exerted to obtain greater concessions from Israel; all the attention of U.S. industry was focused on Israel's access to the U.S. market. Although domestic industry pressure to access foreign markets is typically small compared to the pressure from industry groups interested in minimizing imports, it does serve to mitigate the tendency to maintain the existing structure of protection.

This study also raises a number of important questions
that invite further research on the U.S. trade policy
process. A theoretical question that remains unresolved
in the literature is the causality of protection. While
clearly the pressures in the system maintain the
existing structure of protection, high levels of
protection reflect underlying political pressure or
economic considerations. High tariffs are often a
residual of past economic conditions, such as labor
adjustment costs. These tariffs are maintained because
of political pressure, long after the original economic
conditions have changed. It is still not clear,
however, whether industries become politically visible
because of their ability to exert political pressure or
by virtue of a genuine need. Is the ability of these
industries to organize in turn fueled by their political
visibility, and does the ensuing protection lead to a
growing inability to compete, thus perpetuating this
cycle? Increased research is needed into the determinants of protection, and the extent to which it arises
from political pressures as opposed to economic
considerations.

This study also highlights the need for an examination

of the elements in the U.S. trade policy process that encourage the status quo in terms of protection. The desirability of making changes in the system which would encourage movement away from the existing structure of protection should also be explored. A historic example of a change in the trade policy system occurred after the Smoot-Hawley tariff act was imposed. Before that time Congress was in charge of determining all specific tariff levels. With Smoot-Hawley, and the resulting economic backlash, it was determined that Congress was too subject to constituent pressure to play that role. Institutional changes were made that significantly reduced the ability of pressure groups to influence the level of protection levels in particular industries. These changes involved granting the President the authority to modify tariff levels on particular items within a certain range, and the gradual changing of the ITC from an information gathering agency to a semi-judicial agency with a greater role in determining industry-specific protection. These changes were successful because the President and the ITC are less vulnerable to industry-specific political pressures than the members of Congress.

Other changes in the trade policy process may facilitate changing existing patterns of protection. One potential problems stems from the diversification of trade issues among several Congressional committees. Trade agreements today address an increasingly wide range of non-tariff measures which will involve Congressional committees other than the House Ways and Means Committee and the Senate Finance Committee, which have traditionally had sole jurisdiction over trade agreements. The Committee on Energy and Commerce and Committee on Foreign Affairs became involved in the approval of the Trade and Tariff Act of 1984. Will the requirement that the President consult with every Congressional committee with jurisdiction over matters affected by a trade agreement create jurisdictional disputes that will hamper the implementation of trade legislation, and hinder the efforts of U.S. negotiators by imposing the competing demands of several Congressional committees?[2] While the negotiation of the U.S.-Israel FTA was fraught with obstacles, the fact that a free trade area agreement was successfully concluded represents the hope and promise of future trade liberalizing agreements. Significant symbolic, if not economic, progress was achieved with the negotiation of the U.S.-Israel FTA. It should be emphasized that this represents the first time that the U.S. agreed to eliminate tariffs across

---

[2]Baldwin, The Political Economy of U.S. Import Policy, p.202.

the board under any circumstances. Although tariffs were not the major barriers to trade between the U.S. and Israel, this modest step is significant because it sets the stage for future progress and establishes new norms for international trade agreements. With a rising specter of protectionism, such modest progress is, in the final analysis, an important victory.

VIII. Bibliography

Anderson, Kym, and Baldwin, Robert E. "The Political
Market for Protection in Industrial Countries:
Empirical Evidence," World Bank Staff Working
Paper No.42, October 1981.

Anthony, Beryl, Congressman. Letter to U.S. Trade
Representative William E. Brock, March 7, 1984.
Letter in possession of the Office of the U.S.
Trade Representative, Washington D.C.

Balassa, Bela. "Trade Creation and Diversion in the
European Common Market. An Appraisal of the
Evidence," in European Economic Integration, ed.,
Bela Balassa. Amsterdam: North Holland Publishing
Co., 1975.

Baldwin, Robert E. "Tariff-Cutting Techniques in the
Kennedy Round," in Trade, Growth, and the Balance
of Payments, eds., R.E. Caves, H.G. Johnson, and
P.B. Kennen. Chicago: Rand McNally, 1965.

_____. "The Political Economy of Postwar U.S. Trade
Policy," The Bulletin, New York University Graduate
School of Business Administration, No.4, 1976.

_____. "U.S. Political Pressures Against Adjustment to
Greater Imports," in Trade and Growth of the
Advanced Developing Countries in the Pacific Basin,
eds., Wontack Hong and Lawrence B. Krause.
Seoul: Korea Development Institute, 1981.

_____. "Trade Policies in Developed Countries," in
Handbook of International Economics, vol. I, eds.,
R.W. Jones and P.B. Kennen. Amsterdam: North
Holland Publishing Co., 1984.

_____. The Political Economy of U.S. Import
Protection, Cambridge: Massachusetts Institute of
Technology Press, 1985.

_____, and Wayne E. Lewis. "U.S. Tariff Effects on
Trade and Employment in Detailed SIC Industries,"
in The Impact of International Trade and Investment on Employment, ed., W.G. Dewald. Washington
D.C.: U.S. Department of Labor, 1978.

_____, and John H. Mutti, and J. David Richardson. "Welfare Effects on the U.S. of a Significant Tariff Reduction," Journal of International Economics, vol. 10, 1980.

Bauer, Raymond, Ithiel de Sola Pool, and L. A. Dexter. American Business and Public Policy, New York: Atherton Press, 1963.

Blair, Peggy. "A U.S.-Israel Free Trade Area: How Both Sides Gain," American Israel Public Affairs Committee papers on U.S.-Israel Relations, No.9, Washington D.C., 1984.

Breton, Albert. The Economic Theory of Representative Government, Chicago: Aldine Publishing Co., 1974.

Brock, William A., and Stephen Magee. "Tariff Formation in a Democracy", in Current Issues in Commercial Policy and Diplomacy, eds., John Black and Brian Hindley. London: Macmillan Press, 1980.

_____. "An Economic Theory of Politics: The Case of Tariffs", (mimeographed) 1974, as cited in "The Political Economy of Postwar U.S. Trade Policy," Robert Baldwin. The Bulletin, New York University Graduate School of Business Administration, No.4, 1976.

Brock, William E., former U.S. Trade Representative. Letter to U.S. International Trade Commission Chairman Alfred Eckes, January 25, 1984. Letter in possession of the U.S. International Trade Commission, Washington D.C.

Bruno, Michael, and Stanley Fischer. "The Inflationary Process: Shocks and Accommodation," in The Israeli Economy: Maturing through Crises, ed. Yoram Ben-Porath. Cambridge: Harvard University Press, 1986.

Caves, Richard E. "Economic Models of Political Choice: Canada's Tariff Structure," Canadian Journal of Economics, Vol.9, No.2.

_____, and Ronald W. Jones. World Trade and Payments: An Introduction, Boston: Little, Brown and Co., 1973.

Cairnes, James E. Some Leading Principles in Political Economy, London: Macmillan Press, 1874.

Central Bureau of Statistics. <u>Statistical Abstract of Israel 1969</u>, Government of Israel Publications, No. 20, Jerusalem, 1969.

_____. <u>Statistical Abstract of Israel 1975</u>, Government of Israel Publications, No. 26, Jerusalem, 1975.

_____. <u>Statistical Abstract of Israel 1980</u>, Government of Israel Publications, No. 31, Jerusalem, 1980.

_____. <u>Statistical Abstract of Israel 1982</u>, Government of Israel Publications, No. 33, Jerusalem, 1982.

_____. <u>Statistical Abstract of Israel 1984</u>, Government of Israel Publications, No. 35, Jerusalem, 1984.

Cheh, John. "United States Concessions in the Kennedy Round and Short-Run Labor Adjustment Costs," <u>Journal of International Economics</u>, vol.4, 1974.

Cohen, Yaacov. "Israel and the EEC, 1958-1978: Economic and Political Relations," in <u>The Economic Integration of Israel in the EEC</u>, ed. Herbert Giersch. Tubingen: J.C.B. Mohr (Paul Siebeck), 1980.

Cooper, Doral. "Free Trade Areas: New Opportunities, New Risks," interview in <u>International Business Review</u>, March 1984.

Cooper, Doral, and Nancy Adams. "Overview of the U.S.-Israel Free Trade Area Negotiations: An American Perspective," in a forthcoming book, eds. A. Samet and M. Goldberg. Washington D.C.: International Law Institute, 1988.

Corden, Max W. <u>Trade Policy and Economic Welfare</u>, London: Oxford University Press, 1974.

Downs, Anthony. <u>An Economic Theory of Democracy</u>, New York: Harper and Brothers, 1957.

Jackson, John H. <u>World Trade and the Law of GATT</u>, New York: Bobbs Merrill Co., 1969.

Johnson, Harry G. "The Cost of Protection and the Scientific Tariff," <u>Journal of Political Economy</u>, vol. 68, No. 4., August 1960.

Lavergne, R.P. <u>The Political Economy of U.S. Tarrifs</u>, New York: Academic Press, 1983.

Maddala, G.S. Limited Dependent and Qualitative
    Variables in Econometrics, Cambridge: Cambridge
    University Press, 1983.

McKelvey, Richard, and William Zavolina. "A Statistical
    Model for the Analysis of Ordinal Level Dependent
    Variables," Journal of Mathematical Sociology,
    Summer 1975.

Office of the U.S. Trade Representative. "Summary of
    the U.S.-Israel Free Trade Area Agreement,"
    Unpublished paper, Washington D.C., September 1985.

Olson, Mancur. The Logic of Collective Action,
    Cambridge: Harvard University Press, 1965.

_____. "The Political Economy of Comparative Growth
    Rates," (mimeographed) 1979, as cited in "The
    Political Market for Protection in Industrial
    Countries: Empirical Evidence," Kym Anderson and
    Robert Baldwin. World Bank Staff Working Paper
    No.42, Washington D.C., October 1981.

Pastor, Robert A. Congress and the Politics of
    U.S. Foreign Economic Policy 1929-1976,
    Los Angeles: University of California Press, 1980.

Peltzman, S. "Toward a More General Theory of Regu-
    lation," Journal of Law and Economics, vol.19,
    1976.

Pelzman, Joseph. "The Impact of the U.S.-Israel Free
    Trade Area Agreement on Israeli Trade and Employ-
    ment," The Maurice Falk Institute for Economic
    Research in Israel, Discussion Paper No. 85.08,
    Jerusalem, June 1985. Also published in Israel
    Faces the Future, eds., Bernard Reich and Gershon
    R. Kieval. New York: Praeger Publishers, 1986.

Pincus, Jonathan J. "Pressure Groups and the Pattern of
    Tariffs," Journal of Political Economy, Vol. 83,
    No.4, 1975.

Pindyck, Robert S., and Daniel L. Rubinfeld.
    Econometric Models and Economic Forecasting,
    New York: McGraw-Hill Book Company, 1981.

Platt, Alexander H. "Free Trade With Israel: A
    Legislative History," in a forthcoming book,
    eds., A. Samet and M. Goldberg. Washington
    D.C.: International Law Institute, 1988.

Pomfret, Richard. <u>Trade Policies and Industrialization in a Small Country: The Case of Israel</u>, Tubingen: Kieler Studien, 141, 1976.

_____, and Benjamin Toren. <u>Israel and the European Common Market: An Appraisal of the 1975 Free Trade Agreement</u>, Tubingen: J.C.B. Mohr (Paul Siebeck), 1980.

Riedel, James. "Tariff Concessions in the Kennedy Round and the Structure of Protection in West Germany," <u>Journal of International Economics</u>, vol.7, 1977.

_____. "United States Trade Policy: From Multi-lateralism to Bilateralism?" in <u>Free Trade in the World Economy</u>, ed., Herbert Giersch. Tubingen: J.C.B. Mohr (Paul Siebeck) 1987.

Robson, Peter. <u>The Economics of International Integration</u>, London: Policy Studies Institute, London, 1984.

Sawyer, W. Charles, and Richard Sprinkle. "The Trade Expansion Effects of the U.S.-Israel Free Trade Area Agreement," forthcoming in the Journal of World Trade Law.

Schattschneider, E.E. <u>Politics, Pressures, and the Tariff: A Study of Free Enterprise in Pressure Politics, as Shown in the 1929-1930 Revision of the Tariff</u>, New York: Prentice-Hall, Inc., 1935.

Sellekaerts, W. "How Meaningful are Empirical Studies on Trade Creation and Diversion?" <u>Weltwirtschaftliches Archiv</u> 109, 1973.

Stern, R., A. Deardorff, and C. Shiells. "Estimates of the Elasticities of Substitution Between Imports and Home Goods for the United States," Office of Foreign Economic Research, U.S. Department of Labor, Washington D.C. 1982.

Stigler, George J. "The Economic Theory of Regulation," in <u>The Citizen and the State</u>, Chicago: University of Chicago Press, 1975.

Stolper, W., and Paul A. Samuelson, "Protection and Real Wages," <u>Review of Economic Studies</u>, No. 9, November 1941.

Truman, David B. The Governmental Process, New York; Alfred Knopf, 1971.

Tumlir, Jan. Protectionism: Trade Policy in Democratic Societies, Washington D.C.: American Enterprise Institute, 1985.

U.S. Congress. "The Trade Act of 1974," Public Law 93-618, 93rd Congress, 2nd. Sess., Washington D.C., January 3, 1975.

_____, House Ways and Means Committee, Subcommittee on Trade. "Proposed United States-Israel Free Trade Area," 98th Congress, 2nd. Sess., Washington D.C., May 22, 1984; and June 13, 14, 1984.

_____, Conference Committee. "Conference Report on the Trade and Tariff Act of 1984," 98th Congress, 2nd. Sess., Washington D.C., October 5, 1984.

_____, Senate Finance Committee. "Proposed United States-Israel Free Trade Agreement," 99th Congress, 1st. Sess., Washington D.C., March 20, 1985.

U.S. Department of Labor. "Employment Impact of the U.S.-Israel Free Trade Area: Preliminary Esti mates," Unpublished paper, Washington D.C., November 15, 1984.

U.S. Government Printing Office. "Agreement on the Establishment of a Free Trade Area Between the Government of Israel and the Government of the United States of America," Washington D.C., 1985.

U.S. International Trade Commission. "Fresh Cut Roses from Colombia," Investigation No. 731-TA-148 (preliminary), Washington D.C., November 1983.

_____. "Probable Economic Effect of Providing Duty-Free Treatment for Imports from Israel," Investigation No. 332-180, Washington D.C., May 1984.

List of Interviews

Adams, Nancy, Director of Middle East Affairs, Office of
    the U.S. Trade Representative. Interview by
    author, Washington D.C., July 31, 1985, and
    September 5, 1985.

Anderson, Eve, Industry Analyst, Office of International
    Textile Agreements, U.S. Department of Commerce.
    Telephone interview by author, Washington D.C.,
    August 6, 1985.

Aske, Thelma, Staff member, House Ways and Means
    Committee, Subcommittee on Trade. Interview by
    author, Washington D.C., January 18, 1985.

Bailey, Norman, former Special Assistant on Inter-
    national Trade, National Security Council.
    Interview by author, Washington D.C.,
    January 10, 1985.

Cohen, Shmuel, Assistant to the Deputy Director General
    for Foreign Trade, Ministry of Agriculture. Inter-
    view by author, Tel Aviv, May 16, 1985.

Cohen, Gabriela, International Economist, Office of
    North American Affairs, Ministry of International
    Trade and Industry. Interview by author, Jerusalem,
    May 15, 1985.

Cooper, Doral, Assistant U.S. Trade Representative
    for Asia, Africa and the Pacific, Office of the
    U.S. Trade Representative. Interview by author,
    Washington D.C., January 9, 1985.

Eiss, Don, Senior Policy Analyst, U.S. Department
    of Commerce. Interview by author, Washington D.C.,
    July 25, 1985.

Elhanani, Smadar, Economist, Knesset Finance Committee.
    Interview by author, Jerusalem, May 14, 1985.

Kemp, Geoffrey, former Director of Middle East Affairs,
    National Security Council. Interview by author,
    Washington D.C., January 16, 1985.

Nahum, Moshe, Director of International Trade, Manu-
    facturer's Association of Israel. Interview by
    author, Tel Aviv, March 20, 1985.

Platt, Alexander, former Associate General Counsel, Office of the U.S. Trade Representative. Interview by author, Washington D.C., March 22, 1986.

Pritchard, Dewey, International Economist, U.S. Department of Agriculture. Interview by author, Washington D.C., March 25, 1986.

Radoshitzky, Yoram, Chairman of the Textile Board, Manufacturer's Association of Israel. Interview by author, Tel Aviv, May 23, 1985.

Sorini, Ron, International Economist, Office of Textile Negotiations, Office of the U.S. Trade Representative. Interview by author, Washington D.C., April 2, 1986.

Schoephle, Gregory, International Economist, U.S. Department of Labor. Interview by author, Washington D.C., August 15, 1985.

Semadar, Moshe, former Director for North American Affairs, Ministry of International Trade and Industry. Interview by author, Jerusalem, May 6, 1985.

Wignot, Mary Jane, Staff Director, House Ways and Means Committee, Subcommittee on Trade. Interview by author, Washington D.C., January 14, 1985.

For Product Safety Concerns and Information please contact our EU
representative GPSR@taylorandfrancis.com Taylor & Francis Verlag GmbH,
Kaufingerstraße 24, 80331 München, Germany

Printed and bound by CPI Group (UK) Ltd, Croydon, CR0 4YY
08/05/2025
01864412-0006